NUCLEAR THREAT IN THE MIDDLE EAST

NUCLEAR THREAT IN THE MIDDLE EAST

Robert J. Pranger
Dale R. Tahtinen

American Enterprise Institute for Public Policy Research
Washington, D. C.

Robert J. Pranger and Dale R. Tahtinen are, respectively, director and assistant director of foreign and defense policy studies at the American Enterprise Institute for Public Policy Research.

3 55. 4307

P88 N

94414

Sept 1975

ISBN 0-8447-3172-2

Foreign Affairs Study No. 23, July 1975

Library of Congress Catalog Card No. 75-16306

Printed in the United States of America

CONTENTS

PREFACE

This study is an effort at foresight rather than hindsight. It does not argue that nuclear war in the Middle East is inevitable, nor even suggest that a fifth round of conventional warfare is inescapable. It is written from the standpoint that the best national security option for the United States, the Soviet Union, the Arab countries, and Israel is a just and lasting peace settlement at the earliest possible date. It is our view that such peace is possible and probably more likely than the matter covered in this study. We also believe that unless the utmost in human resourcefulness is demonstrated, this peace will not be achieved. In the absence of peace, the engines of war will continue to move toward higher levels of technical sophistication. For modern defense planning the ultimate in technological achievement is atomic weaponry.

This study looks toward the worst imaginable case in which warfare continues and escalates into the use of nuclear weapons. We have adopted a central hypothesis: if war is not curbed in the Middle East, it will eventually become nuclear. This estimate is at least as plausible as forecasts of an oil war. And we ask the following four questions to test our hypothesis:

- Is nuclear war possible in the Middle East?
- Do nuclear weapons now exist in the Middle East?
- What types of military equipment in the Middle East are capable of delivering nuclear weapons?
- What are some possible scenarios for the use of nuclear and chemical-biological weapons in the Middle East?

These questions dealt with, we examine a plan for an American response to nuclear war in the Middle East—parts of which we hope will never have to be used.

Robert J. Pranger
Dale R. Tahtinen
June 1975

1
IS NUCLEAR WAR POSSIBLE IN THE MIDDLE EAST?

An elaborate but largely unwritten code of conduct, by no means automatic in its operation, separates and yet unites the nuclear defenses of the United States and the Soviet Union. Without avowing similar global strategies, the two superpowers have learned to live in an uneasy equilibrium based on foreknowledge of certain mass destruction if they should engage in full-scale general war. The code separating and uniting them has evolved by mutual, tacit consent since the first Russian atomic explosion in 1949 (before which only the United States had nuclear weapons), under the realization that future total wars between great powers will bear no resemblance to those of the past. There will be no prolonged combat, save possibly something resembling the spasmodic death throes of a giant prehistoric beast. The term total war will achieve new meaning under radically different circumstances, with emphasis on the totality of immediate destruction rather than the art of long campaigns.

So obvious is this code of nuclear conduct—often called "deterrence"—that no more than a rudimentary description of it need be given. First, the understanding between the two superpowers, while not symmetrical in strategic terms, is mutual in political terms. Motives and aims may be ambiguous, but the possible consequences of using atomic war as an instrument of international policy are unmistakably clear. Second, the vocabulary of deterrence is shared, even in the context of radically different national values. Central to this lexicon is the concept of retaliation should one superpower attack the other first. Related are terms such as escalation and survival, designed to underline the impression, backed by awesome reality, of vast potential force. Third, the technology of retaliation results in a kind of similarity between the two strategic nuclear forces, which emphasizes the dire consequences of total war. And fourth, political understanding, deterrence rhetoric, and weapons technology have all been "encoded" as a result of numerous direct consultations between the United States and the U.S.S.R in times of crisis.

In other words, policy, rhetoric, technology and communication provide important elements in a common code for nuclear behavior between the two superpowers. This code tends to create an impression of rationality in the general war policies of Moscow and Washington, even though these giants frequently complain about threats from each other, and despite persistent arguments by some critics that this rationality is specious. Proponents and opponents of nuclear preparedness alike often refer to this code as a "balance of terror," but such labelling sometimes obscures the very careful and continuous effort that underlies the equilibrium of nuclear forces between the United States and the Soviet Union.[1] National defense of this magnitude is hardly conceived and operated by terrorists, but instead by responsible human beings. Of course, this responsibility does not diminish the potential danger of such defense.

The very evolution of this joint code of nuclear behavior between Russia and America has exercised both salutary and unhealthy influences on a broad range of bilateral relations. Most surely the buildup and perfection of nuclear weapons has added a sobering picture of the potentials of war policy in the field of contemporary foreign affairs. At the same time, however, the dynamism of technological change tends to strain against the human limits of policy and communication, thus producing among two powers already having enormous problems communicating with each other a certain anxiety over status within the nuclear equilibrium. Through such anxiety a form of terror may well develop, but hardly anything producing a "balance." Quite the contrary, with terror may come irrational, unbalanced behavior, a danger all the more possible since it is always clearly understood that the code of mutual good conduct in nuclear matters does not in any way contain or dispel the fundamental adversary relationships between the two powers.

Nonetheless, a bilateral code for regulating nuclear defense has developed. Whether a given period in Russo-American relations is called détente or cold war, both sides assume that a sense of nuclear equilibrium, together with balanced thinking on military matters, will be maintained. And they most surely perceive that it will be within the immediate considerations of this code, and not out of certain political animosities transcending it, that decisions to use nuclear

---

[1] See Albert Wohlstetter, "The Delicate Balance of Terror," *Foreign Affairs,* vol. 37, no. 2 (January 1959), pp. 211-234.

weapons will be made, if indeed they are ever made. There is no question that the retaliatory code would be the controlling factor in any use of nuclear weapons. It would be the ultimate arbiter in favor or against actual employment of such weapons. Probabilities would have to be calculated within a set of constraints that have evolved in mutually recognized but tacit rules of military behavior.

The most dangerous element in nuclear proliferation among nations outside the realm of this web of policy, deterrence, technology and communication between Moscow and Washington is that beyond this almost ritualized, bilateral relationship there is no ritual and, in certain instances, not even bilateral relations. In the Middle East no significant formal or informal relationships between the Arab governments and Israel exist, to say nothing of a code for nuclear conduct should such weapons be introduced into this tumultuous setting. Yet there are indications mounting in their persuasiveness that such weapons may already be present in the region, while most surely the capability to build and deliver nuclear ordnance has expanded. It may well be that nuclear weapons will be used in the Middle East in the near future, perhaps even in the next round of fighting, should there be another war. If so, this will occur in the complete absence of diplomatic relations for crisis management between Jerusalem and the Arab capitals and between Jerusalem and Moscow, to say nothing of a code of carefully evolved regulations on nuclear warfare that at once separate and unite these adversaries so as to keep them from all but certain mutual destruction.

The nuclear scenarios that follow, as well as possible developments in the areas of chemical and biological warfare, are not exaggerated. If the capability to build such weapons now exists in the Middle East, with a fairly strong probability that stockpiling has already commenced in Israel, then one might expect they will be used under certain circumstances barring any unwritten rules for constraining their employment against hated adversaries. This is made all the more probable by the supply by the major powers of a wide range of air, land and maritime vehicles capable of launching nuclear ordnance (as well as some indigenously constructed models), capacities resulting either from the "dual capability" of certain weapons (as with the American F-4 and Soviet MiG-23 fighter-bombers) or from primarily nuclear-oriented systems (as with the American Lance missile recently offered for sale to Israel).

In the nuclear code of conduct separating the United States and the Soviet Union there are certain provisions for how each should act if nuclear weapons are used by third parties. The one surprise development at the 1973 Nixon-Brezhnev summit meeting in Washington was a mutual pledge to curb third-party use of nuclear weapons and to warn each other should such employment be expected.[2] But the rules of behavior on this point are sketchy at best and surely open to controversies over good faith (see a further analysis of the agreement's limitations in Chapter 5 below). Consequently, should powers not under any restraints actually use nuclear weapons against each other or threaten use against one of the superpowers, one of the least perfected areas of the code between Moscow and Washington would become operative—a code principally designed for bilateral military relations—that of third-party nuclear warfare. Leaving aside possible recriminations, there is an outside chance that the Moscow-Washington nuclear equilibrium might itself break down as the political relations between the two deteriorate over such incidents. No more so would this chain reaction from policy conflict to nuclear anxiety be likely to happen than in the Middle East, where the two superpowers have often clashed politically and occasionally brushed each other with military force. Given the rather strong military assurances already tendered the Arab states and Israel by their respective patrons, commitments that may or may not have included hints of a nuclear umbrella,[3] such dangerous developments are all the more possible. Surely the partial worldwide alert of U.S. strategic forces in the 1973 Middle East war would give some credence to the idea that there is an American nuclear umbrella over Israel, although as an outgrowth of the breakdown in the 1975 peace talks, U.S. policy toward the Middle East is said to be under reassessment.

In summary, the possibility of nuclear war between the United States and the Soviet Union has been governed to a considerable extent by a military code of nuclear conduct that stands outside of their diplomatic relations, whether these relations be exacerbated or amicable at any given time. Such codes apparently do not exist between other present or potential nuclear powers, or between the superpowers and others armed with atomic weaponry, except as special alliance considerations may supervene. These rules are most definitely not present among regional adversaries in the Middle East, as indeed

---

[2] "Agreement between the United States of America and the Union of Soviet Socialist Republics on the Prevention of Nuclear War," 22 June 1973, in U.S. Department of State, *Department of State Bulletin*, vol. 69, no. 1778 (23 July 1973), pp. 160-161.

[3] "In 1962 President Kennedy assured [then] Foreign Minister Meir that the United States and Israel were *de facto* allies. The following year a written assurance from Kennedy to [Prime Minister] Eshkol contained a virtual guarantee of Israel's territorial integrity." Michael Brecher, *Decisions in Israel's Foreign Policy* (New Haven: Yale University Press, 1975), p. 322.

not even diplomacy exercises its limited restraints between Israel and the Arab states. And the relations governing nuclear policy between Moscow and Washington extend only tentatively to third-party usage, even while superpower nuclear umbrellas may cover some of these same parties. The result of all these considerations, and especially the current arms supply policies of the superpowers, is that possible nuclear scenarios for actual use in the Middle East must be considered plausible. The language and practice of deterrence has little or no meaning between Arabs and Israelis.[4] It is to the probable existence of nuclear weapons in the Middle East, to nuclear delivery vehicles in the region, to possible nuclear and other unconventional (chemical-biological weapons) scenarios, and to the American response to such eventualities that this study now turns.

---

[4] A case for a stable nuclear balance—and hence deterrence—between Arabs and Israelis has been made by Steven J. Rosen, of Australian National University, in his unpublished paper "Nuclearization and Stability in the Middle East" (1975). The purpose of his analysis is to explore the consequences of actual deployment of nuclear weapons in the Middle East. Rosen notes, in Israel's political-military thinking on nuclear weapons, important opposition to relying on such an arsenal.

2
DO NUCLEAR WEAPONS NOW EXIST IN THE MIDDLE EAST?

Fred Charles Iklé, director of the U.S. Arms Control and Disarmament Agency, has recently warned that nuclear weapons proliferation will ride on the shoulders of national commitments to peaceful uses of atomic energy.[1] This suggests that the spread of nuclear technology for laudable human goals displays the usual ethical ambiguity of such technology: the *uses* are often not predetermined but flow instead from choices about how knowledge will be applied. Nuclear technology, in and of itself, is not the main driving force for the spread of atomic weapons, even though it provides the base upon which decisions for peaceful *and* military uses might develop.

If decisions made on the basis of a technology already under way are the central determinants of whether or not a country builds nuclear weapons, then the causes of such decisions may well be, in part at least, extraneous to simple possession of such technological capability in the first place. What determines the military exploitation of this capacity? For some states, a decision to build nuclear weapons and deploy them may emerge from a desire to possess a modern military force appropriate to great powers, even if there seems no immediate danger of atomic attack. France may well fit into this category. Certain nations might feel an immediate threat from other nuclear powers and determine that their only salvation is in a credible nuclear force of their own. This view underlies the present nuclear equilibrium between the United States and the Soviet

---

[1] Leslie H. Gelb, "Arms Expert Warns on Nuclear Spread," *New York Times,* 10 April 1975; and Mason Willrich, "Nuclear Power Development and Nuclear Weapon Proliferation," in Anne W. Marks, ed., *NPT: Paradoxes and Problems* (Washington, D. C.: Arms Control Association—Carnegie Endowment for International Peace, 1975), pp. 55-73. Concern may grow with the development of laser isotope-enrichment techniques (see below).

Union and probably is responsible for China's strategic forces program. India may fit this category, too, although something like the French case is present there as well. A third class of nation may actually be engaged in conventional hostilities with others and be simultaneously developing nuclear weapons on a contingency basis, either for deterrence should some occasion require a strong threat or for use in the event all else fails. The fact that such development takes place in the midst of war, however, is significant because there will probably be fewer constraints during hostilities than in the absence of war. This third situation was that of the United States in the Second World War, and it is now probably that of the Middle East nations.

Iklé's warning, coupled with some sensitivity as to what are basic reasons for decisions to use peaceful technology for military purposes, can be applied to the Middle East. Fundamentally, any capacity for nuclear weapons in this region will appear under the guise and in the van of "peaceful uses" of atomic energy. Any country both at war and equipped with nuclear technology apparently not diverted to this war, should be placed in the category of a potential nuclear military power. Both Egyptians and Israelis have said as much about themselves.[2] Programs of research and other peaceful applications of nuclear energy have been under way for some time in Egypt, Iraq and Israel. Iran and perhaps others will soon join this club. As we will note further below, while it has been previously thought that the absence of large enough quantities of plutonium would prevent the development of nuclear arms in the Middle East, the new technology of laser enrichment of uranium has undergone one of its most significant advances in Israel.[3] Also, mystery surrounds certain current operations in at least one Middle East reactor center, Israel's Dimona facility. And finally, there will be a steady expansion of atomic facilities throughout the region.

---

[2] See Israeli President Efraim Katzir's statement of 1 December 1974 that "Israel has a nuclear potential," quoted from *Ma'ariv* (2 December 1974), by Foreign Broadcast Information Service (FBIS) in FBIS-MEA-74-233, 3 December 1974, p. N 1. Also, Egyptian President Anwar as-Sadat's interview with the Etelaat newspaper chain in Iran, 17 December 1974: "If Israel introduces atomic weapons into the area, we will find a means to have them, too." Sadat quote in John K. Cooley, "Egypt Seen Assessing Nuclear Strength," *Christian Science Monitor*, 2 January 1975.

[3] Robert Gillette, "Uranium Enrichment: Rumors of Israeli Progress with Lasers," *Science*, vol. 183, no. 4130 (22 March 1974), pp. 1172-1174. Progress in laser isotope enrichment has also been driving forward in the U.S. and the U.S.S.R. See Walter Sullivan, "U.S. Lab [Los Alamos] Develops a Laser Technique that May Facilitate Atom Arms Output," *New York Times*, 24 April 1975.

In addition to the growing technological base for nuclear power, both peaceful and military, the course of events in the Middle East continues to produce the kinds of anxieties that make for heavy defense expenditure and intense curiosity about more sophisticated means of warfare. This is another way of saying that the fiction of "no-war, no-peace" masks an unpleasant reality: like the Austrian Emperor Franz on the eve of Metternich's decision to stage a final military showdown with Napoleon, the parties talk "peace, lasting peace" and prepare for war should their "reasonable" demands be refused.[4] Under these circumstances, conditions are propitious for making decisions to divert nuclear technology in the Middle East, at least in part, to military uses.

It should be noted that this war preparation is not the same kind of "deterrence" operating between the United States and the Soviet Union (which makes it especially unwise for the nuclear superpowers to entangle their defense strategies with events in the Middle East). Regardless of the vitriolic propaganda battles waged during the cold war, an elementary fact stands out in superpower relations: scarcely a shot has been fired in anger since the early 1920s. Indeed, as much as the U.S.S.R. has consistently hidden the historical experience, the two giants have actually collaborated rather closely on military matters, both during World War II and even in the informal deterrence code referred to earlier in this study.

In stark contrast, relations between Israel and the Arabs have been marked by four major wars in twenty-five years, with almost constant violence preceding Israel's independence in 1948 and with periods of sporadic fighting between all wars since. No diplomatic relations or any other kind of direct official contacts exist between Jerusalem and its Arab neighbors. Even the more moderate Arabs, such as President Anwar as-Sadat of Egypt, insist that one should expect no direct relations of any importance with Israel during the generation of present Arab leadership. Needless to say, Israeli and Arab perceptions of each other's credibility are abysmally low when it comes to peaceful intentions, but on the subject of warlike designs all are agreed that even the most blatant threat is not half as bad as what the enemy actually intends.

While it may be frightening to some that nuclear weapons could be introduced into this setting, it is precisely such an atmosphere that would generate the introduction and use of such weapons. The

---

[4] On the events of the summer of 1813, see Henry A. Kissinger, *A World Restored: The Politics of Conservatism in a Revolutionary Age* (New York: Grosset & Dunlap—The Universal Library, 1964), p. 80.

American decision to build atomic ordnance was made during the heat of battle in World War II, for *use* against the hated Nazis (who were defeated before such weapons were necessary) and then for *use* against the Japanese to save *American* lives that might otherwise have been lost in an invasion of Japan proper.[5] Such niceties as nuclear balance, deterrence theory and so forth have come into play only after the Russians began to build their own atomic weapons, for reasons no less anxious than ours, and it then became apparent by the mid-1950s that any use of nuclear weapons by either super-power against the other would spell mutual disaster. But the on-going evolution of a nuclear code of good conduct between Moscow and Washington has been aided by the fact that, despite all the Sturm und Drang in their relations, the ideological war between capitalism and communism has not occasioned overt military hostilities between the two countries since the Russian civil war. Some might argue that this outbreak was prevented or "deterred" by the presence of nuclear weapons—the peace-through-strength argument—but whatever the reason, a code developed in the absence of war, not in its presence. Actual use of nuclear weapons by the United States, as well as the decision to build them in the first place, came during World War II and the American absorption with a grotesque fascist enemy.

The Middle East situation today is more analogous to conditions during World War II, for there has been warfare or the real threat of warfare in the region for twenty-five years. While some attention has been drawn during this time to the cold war's influence on Middle Eastern affairs, the context of war between Israel and the Arabs has been uniquely their own. As a consequence of the strong holocaust fixation of the Israeli leadership, conditions were not only analogous to the Second World War, they "were" that war, replayed in the struggle with the Arabs.[6] Hence, efforts to apply doctrines of military rationality (or perhaps any kind of rationality) to nuclear developments in the Middle East must be seen in light of wartime exigencies and not in the pseudo-violence of ideological warfare.

---

[5] Harry S. Truman, *Memoirs by Harry S. Truman*, 2 vols. (Garden City, N. Y.: Doubleday, 1955, 1956), vol. 1, pp. 415-423.

[6] "The Holocaust fixation has pervaded Israel's foreign policy since independence. Justifiable in the early years, it began to lose credibility after the Sinai Campaign; and in 1970 . . . Israel was the strongest actor in the area, amply capable of surviving an Arab attack. The [belief of Prime Minister Golda] Meir . . . , widely shared among Israel's decisionmakers, was a major psychological obstacle to intelligent and efficient decision-making." Brecher, *Decisions in Israel's Foreign Policy*, p. 514 (with reference to the Rogers proposals of 1969-1970). See also pp. 333-335, 342-343 on Six-Day War of 1967 and "Holocaust syndrome."

"In war more than anywhere else in the world," Clausewitz noted, "things happen differently to what we had expected, and look differently when near, to what they did at a distance."[7] One may recall that when it appeared that Japan, not Germany, would be the likely first target for an American atomic bomb, the decision to drop it was pressed for quite different reasons than originally expected: it was not dropped because the Japanese might have similar weapons (the initial rationale for building them against Nazi Germany), but because we had them and they did not, thus making the outcome definitive.

This discussion of technological base and political-military choices is necessary in order to establish ground rules for the evidence that follows. Some of the facts are circumstantial, others less ambiguous. But the point really is not absolute proof for the existence of nuclear weapons in the Middle East, though there are plenty of grounds for such proof. The real issue is whether there are in the Middle East: (1) *necessary* technical capacities to build weapons, and (2) *sufficient* political-military reasons for moving forward on nuclear arms programs. It would be pointless—even mischievous—to probe around in sensitive areas such as this, unless one has reasonably good hunches that both Israel and the Arab states would be moved to engage in building and even using nuclear weapons. A combination of imminent danger, plausible hypotheses and substantial evidence make the subject of nuclear weapons in the Middle East an essential policy issue for the United States.

Evidence of Nuclear Weapons in the Middle East

During the past several years, responsible public sources have addressed themselves to the likelihood that Israel has secretly joined the exclusive club of states possessing nuclear weapons. Israel is known to have at least two reactor centers.[8] The oldest, the Nahal Soreq Research Center, is located just south of Tel Aviv and was purchased from the United States in 1955 under the Atoms for Peace

---

[7] Karl von Clausewitz, *On War*, Book III, Chapter VII, translated by J. J. Graham (1908), edited by Anatol Rapoport (Baltimore: Penguin Books, 1968), p. 263.

[8] Fuad Jabber, *Israel and Nuclear Weapons* (London: Chatto and Windus for the Institute for Strategic Studies, 1971), pp. 25-32. Also, see *The Middle East and North Africa 1972-1973* (London: Europa, 1972), p. 425. Another study has indicated that "Egypt and Syria would . . . be unwise to suppose that Israel could not mount a nuclear attack on a small number of targets." John Maddox, "Prospects for Nuclear Proliferation," *Adelphi Papers*, no. 113 (London: The International Institute for Strategic Studies, 1975), p. 9.

Program.[9] The second, near Dimona in the northern Negev Desert, was built with French assistance on the basis of a 1957 agreement between Paris and Tel Aviv.[10] Of the two reactors, the one near Dimona is more important in a military sense because it is said to be "particularly well-suited for producing the fissionable plutonium used in nuclear bombs."[11] Indeed, this facility is reportedly similar to the American one at Savannah River, South Carolina, which has been the source of a large part of the U.S. plutonium stockpile.[12]

The exact amount of plutonium produced by the Dimona reactor is not known, but there have been several quite similar estimates. It was reported in July 1970 that the reactor's output was enough for about one twenty kiloton bomb per year since 1966.[13] Two years later it was contended that, since its start-up in 1964, the Dimona facility has given Israel the physical capacity to produce enough plutonium to construct a minimum of one Nagasaki-size atomic bomb (nineteen kilotons) annually.[14] At about the same time, it was estimated that Israel already had enough plutonium to make as many as eight bombs.[15]

The existence of facilities such as the Dimona reactor is particularly important because many nuclear physicists believe that most individuals with a Ph.D.—and often less formal training—in the field can make an atomic bomb if the materials are available.[16] Thus, the ability to produce plutonium, coupled with the known expertise of Israeli scientists, tends to demonstrate that Israel does have the capability to build such weapons.[17] In addition, former Central Intelligence Agency Director Richard Helms reportedly told the Senate

---

[9] Jabber, *Nuclear Weapons*, p. 35.

[10] Ibid.

[11] *New York Times*, 20 December 1960. On plutonium produced in nuclear reactors for use as a core material in fission explosions, see Mason Willrich and Theodore B. Taylor, *Nuclear Theft: Risks and Safeguards*, A Report to the Energy Policy Project of the Ford Foundation (Cambridge, Mass.: Ballinger, 1974), pp. 12-16.

[12] *New York Times*, 20 December 1960. Also see Jabber, *Nuclear Weapons*, p. 41.

[13] Hedrick Smith, "U.S. Assumes the Israelis Have A-Bomb or Its Parts," *New York Times*, 18 July 1970.

[14] J. Bowyer Bell, "Israel's Nuclear Option," *The Middle East Journal*, Autumn 1972, p. 382.

[15] *Safeguarding the Atom*, a report of an American panel which met in July 1972 under the auspices of the United Nations Association of the United States of America. One science writer notes: "Israel's tightly guarded reactor at Dimona . . . probably has produced enough plutonium for a bomb or two, but arrangements covering ownership of spent fuel containing the plutonium have never been disclosed." Gillette, "Uranium Enrichment," p. 1174.

[16] See Willrich and Taylor, *Nuclear Theft*, pp. 6-9. Not all agree.

[17] For a more detailed analysis, see Jabber, *Nuclear Weapons*.

Foreign Relations Committee in a closed-door hearing on 7 July 1970 that the American estimate of Israel's nuclear capability was that it has the capacity to build atomic weapons.[18]

CIA interest in the Israeli nuclear program, as well as in atomic weapons development in other states, is not surprising. In fact, on 31 January 1974 an event involving the CIA and a University of Rochester faculty member put the issue of nuclear weapons in the Middle East in new perspective. According to a *Science* account published on 22 March 1974,[19] Michael M. Hercher, an associate professor of optics at Rochester, was approached by a CIA representative with a request that Hercher look over some abstracts of papers and patent applications on tunable lasers. (It is theoretically possible to remove all the uranium 235 from natural uranium by means of laser enrichment of uranium isotopes, at significant savings in the physical size and capital cost of enrichment plants.) Among the abstracts was one describing a laser enrichment process developed by Isaiah Nebenzahl, a physicist with Israel's Ministry of Defense, and Menahem Levin of Tel Aviv University. The same general process has been the subject of considerable research interest in the United States. Exxon Nuclear Inc. is involved in a joint venture with Avco Everett Research Laboratories, and the AEC has been working on it at the Los Alamos Scientific Laboratory and at the Lawrence Livermore Laboratory in California (see footnote 3 above).

A patent for the Nebenzahl-Levin application was sought in West Germany in March 1972 (awarded on 4 October 1973), while Nebenzahl was a post-doctoral research associate at Cornell University. Questions have been raised by Avco officials as to whether there were connections between Avco's staff and Nebenzahl, but apparently there would be nothing dubious in any event since laser isotope separation had been widely discussed since the late 1960s.

A part of the Nebenzahl-Levin abstract seemed especially interesting from the standpoint of Israel's future capabilities to produce nuclear weapons. One should recall that the Dimona and Nahal Soreq reactors would have little capacity for large-scale weapons

---

[18] Smith, "Israelis Have A-Bomb." Also see a report in the *New York Times*, 9 August 1972, on an article from the Soviet newspaper *Moskovski Komsomolyets* which addressed the topic of Israel's nuclear capability. Some have contended that Israel may not be quite so close to actually possessing atomic weapons. See George Quester, *The Politics of Nuclear Proliferation* (Baltimore: Johns Hopkins University Press, 1973), and S. Flapan, "Israel's Attitude Towards the NPT," in *Nuclear Proliferation Problems*, Stockholm International Peace Research Institute (Cambridge: MIT Press, 1974).

[19] Gillette, "Uranium Enrichment," pp. 1172-1174. On high-enriched uranium as core material in a fission bomb, see Willrich and Taylor, *Nuclear Theft*, pp. 16-18.

production. In the words of Robert Gillette, writing the *Science* commentary of 22 March 1974, "the abstract . . . told how, in 24 hours, the process produced a 'yield of 7 grams [of uranium 235] of purity 60 percent.' According to one weapons authority, a clever designer would need just under 50 kilograms of uranium enriched to 60 percent ^{235}U to make a fission bomb." [20]

Xerox copies of the abstract have subsequently circulated in the interested American research communities, through Los Alamos and Livermore and back to Avco and AEC in Washington. "The general reaction appears to have been one of astonishment tinged with disbelief." [21] One laser researcher at Los Alamos is quoted by *Science* as saying, "I guess it means the Israelis are building bombs in their basements." [22] Avco Vice-President Richard H. Levy hoped it was not true, but if true "it's a peculiar way to announce a nuclear weapons program. . . . It shook a lot of us up." [23]

Nebenzahl himself has been careful in his responses to questions. In a telephone interview with *Science*, he apologized for his vagueness, which he said grew out of concern for patent protection rather than national security. He said the work had been carried out in a "government nuclear center." The Israeli physicist maintains that the laser technique is actually "an experiment plus a calculation plus an extrapolation," in answer to a query about whether any amount of uranium 235 had been separated by this method.[24] In other words, there may be something more hypothetical than real about the Israeli technique, or at least this may have been so in 1972 when the patent was applied for.[25]

Nonetheless, Gillette concludes his interesting account in *Science* by underlining the almost inevitable technological erosion of the cost and "conspicuousness" of enriching uranium, and noting that "as a result, smaller and less affluent nations may eventually find their nuclear intentions easier to fulfill and harder for others to discover," even though it is probable, "that no one is yet lasing natural uranium into gram lots of bomb-quality material." [26]

[20] Gillette, "Uranium Enrichment," p. 1174.

[21] Ibid.

[22] Ibid.

[23] Ibid.

[24] Ibid.

[25] Ibid.

[26] Ibid. A similar view is expressed by Willrich and Taylor, as of 1974: ". . . for at least a few more years" laser isotope enrichment facilities "will be extremely costly and complex and probably beyond the reach of any but the highly industrialized nations." Willrich and Taylor, *Nuclear Theft*, p. 18. But see Sullivan, "U.S. Lab Develops a Laser Technique."

If it is likely that the laser-enrichment technique has not only found its way to the Middle East but has been developed there by a scientist attached to the Israeli Ministry of Defense in collaboration with a colleague, then this effort only reinforces an earlier observation. Whether or not the laser technique has actually produced nuclear weapons in Israel, a matter on which the United States government has been notably silent, there does seem to be at least circumstantial evidence that laser-enrichment may have some professional interest to Israel's Ministry of Defense.[27] Hence, technological capability may already have been melded with political-military considerations, the necessary linkage for turning nuclear technology into defense applications. Since the technique would also involve ultimately less expensive and less conspicuous production of uranium 235 for weapons than current processes, the question of large-scale physical evidence of plutonium (or high-enriched uranium), an issue in the past with respect to the Dimona facility, would be largely irrelevant. However, one should note expert testimony to the effect that for the next few years this process may be extremely costly and beyond the reach of all but the most highly industrialized nations.

As important as having the capability, however, is the fact that Israel apparently has been actually building nuclear weapons. On 5 May 1969 it was reported that Israel, using plutonium from the Dimona facility, already had five or six devices about equal in strength to the atomic bomb dropped on Hiroshima (nineteen kilotons) during World War II.[28] Also, in the late 1960s "it was suggested that Israel would have suitable nuclear warheads of its own design available by 1970, produced in the Dimona reactor centre. . . ."[29]

In mid-1970 it was reported that "for at least two years" Washington had been "conducting its Middle East policy on the assumption that Israel either possesses an atomic bomb or has component parts available for quick assembly. . . ."[30] It was said that there had been some disagreement among senior American officials over the conclusiveness of the evidence upon which the assumption was based,

---

[27] The story was brought to wider public attention in Washington by Smith Hempstone in a *Washington Star-News* column of 29 March 1974, "Why Israel Pulled Back" (referring to the disengagement with Egypt). Hempstone noted the Israeli policy of "deterrence through uncertainty" on the question of their nuclear capabilities, vowing on the one hand never to use nuclear weapons first, but at the same time never signing the Treaty on the Non-Proliferation of Nuclear Weapons (NPT).

[28] *Der Spiegel*, 5 May 1969.

[29] John W. R. Taylor, ed., *Jane's All The World's Aircraft 1972-73* (New York: McGraw-Hill, 1972), p. 565.

[30] Smith, "Israelis Have A-Bomb."

15

but those discussions at times supposedly centered on such technicalities as whether a country should be classified as having atomic weapons if the final wire or mechanism was not yet in place.[31] These statements were then followed in 1971 by reports that some analysts were contending Tel Aviv already had the components from which nuclear weapons could rapidly be assembled.[32] At a Jerusalem reception for scientific correspondents on 1 December 1974, Israel's President Efraim Katzir candidly admitted that "Israel has a nuclear potential." He added, apparently in reference to more general weapons development, "We are producing small computers and military components, and we have developed various types of weapons."[33]

In addition to such statements, there are other significant indications that Israel has nuclear weapons. For example, it has been observed that the Jericho missile is too costly to be expended for delivering conventional warheads.[34] Also, when Israel was negotiating for fifty Phantom jets in 1968 its officials reportedly requested that some of the planes be equipped with racks for nuclear bombs.[35] An additional point is that, according to "some knowledgeable sources," in 1968 "fissionable material from the Dimona reactor was diverted from normal peaceful uses and disappeared."[36] The report went on to say, that "it is not known whether this [material] was diverted to weapons use but that is the strong presumption here."[37]

There have also been several political actions by Israel's government that have done little to discourage the assumption that it possesses nuclear weapons. Probably the most significant among them is the censorship that prevents domestic press speculation about nuclear capacity.[38] Another example is Israel's refusal to sign the Treaty on the Non-Proliferation of Nuclear Weapons (NPT). Certainly if the latter action were based on the premise of keeping future options open because of a fear that an Arab nuclear power will arise, then one could reasonably expect Israel to indicate that it will sign the treaty if the two important Arab non-signatories—Algeria and Saudi Arabia—will do the same. Little has been heard, however,

---

31 Ibid.
32 William Beecher, "Watch on Suez: Israel Weighs the Options," *Army*, December 1971, p. 31. Also see his article, "Israel Believed Producing Missile of Atom Capability," *New York Times*, 5 October 1971.
33 As quoted in FBIS-MEA-74-233, 3 December 1974, p. N 1.
34 Beecher, "Israel Believed Producing Missile of Atom Capability."
35 Smith, "Israelis Have A-Bomb."
36 Ibid.
37 Ibid.
38 Bell, "Nuclear Option," p. 381. Also see Jabber, *Nuclear Weapons*.

regarding what conditions are essential before Israel will sign the NPT. In this respect, Egypt has only signed, not ratified, the NPT, making its ratification contingent on Israel's.[39]

As a party to the NPT and presumably under a strong obligation to encourage its friends and allies to sign and ratify the treaty, the United States apparently has taken the position that the NPT need not be a prior condition for American negotiations on nuclear cooperation with Middle East states. At a hearing held by the House Foreign Affairs Subcommittee on the Near East and South Asia on 27 June 1974, the following exchange took place between Representative Jonathan B. Bingham (D.-N.Y.) and Alfred L. Atherton, Jr., assistant secretary of state for Near Eastern and South Asian affairs:

> MR. BINGHAM: . . . You have indicated that it is the policy of the Government to impose the most rigid possible safeguards with respect to the nuclear power plants to be built in Egypt and in Israel. At a recent hearing the representative of the IAEA [International Atomic Energy Agency] indicated that there was no intention of asking the parties to enter into the nonproliferation agreement as a condition which would provide additional safeguards in the view of at least two of our expert witnesses. Do you have any comment on that?
>
> MR. ATHERTON: Only that obviously there is a matter of policy. We encourage all nations to join and ratify the nonproliferation treaty. We have not considered that we should make this a condition for entering into cooperation agreements at the present time. There are many complicated reasons of policy that have prevented certain governments from taking the step. We continue to encourage them to do it but I think one has to have a certain amount of flexibility in approaching that as opposed to the question of the reality of safeguards on which we feel that there cannot be any flexibility so far as the kind of assurances that we feel are going to be central.[40]

The Atherton idea of "flexibility" seems to bear some similarity to an argument made by George H. Quester of Cornell University

---

[39] See statement by President Anwar as-Sadat quoted in FBIS-MEA-75-68, 8 April 1975, p. D 3; from MENA (Cairo, 6 April 1975), in an exclusive press statement made to Wilson Wynn, *Time* magazine bureau chief in Cairo.

[40] U.S. Congress, House, Committee on Foreign Affairs, Subcommittee on the Near East and South Asia, *The Middle East, 1974: New Hopes, New Challenges,* 93rd Congress, 2nd session (Washington, D. C.: U.S. Government Printing Office, 1974), pp. 148-149. It should be noted that while Egypt has signed the NPT, it has not ratified it. Israel has not signed. Consequently, American nuclear assistance to either Egypt or Israel would require that Washington be flexible.

regarding Israel's adherence to the NPT, though in one important respect Atherton's position goes beyond Quester's.[41] Quester notes that arguments for the NPT carry little weight in Israel, since there seem to be few advantages. On the contrary, there are substantial disadvantages to adherence in nuclear research and energy programs. In addition, many Israeli officials see merit in keeping the Arabs guessing. Quester notes that Israel might still sign the treaty, if its reputation and U.S. arms assistance were dependent on it, but American policy makers must weigh marginal advantages and disadvantages in pressing for Israeli commitment. Among possible disadvantages of adherence, from the perspective of curbing nuclear proliferation, is that by ratifying the treaty Israel qualifies for additional assistance in the peaceful uses of atomic energy, which could make clandestine arms manufacture simpler. The Atherton idea of flexibility in cooperative agreements, however, would seem to allow Middle East countries, not parties to the NPT, to have assistance advantages similar to those obtainable under the NPT without having to undergo any of the treaty's restrictions, chief among which is the objective of IAEA safeguards under the NPT: "Timely detection of significant quantities of nuclear material . . . and deterrence of such diversion through the risk of early detection."[42] It might be said that the American approach is something like "having your cake and eating it too" in the field of nuclear development.

Given the blanket of secrecy enshrouding Israel's nuclear activities, it is not surprising that the few official statements from Jerusalem about the status of such weapons development have denied that Israel is a nuclear state.[43] Israeli spokesmen have said that their country will not be the first "to introduce nuclear weapons into the Arab-Israeli conflict."[44] Other recent official statements have indicated that Israel is capable of producing nuclear weapons. For

---

[41] George H. Quester, "Israel and the Nuclear Non-Proliferation Treaty," *Bulletin of the Atomic Scientists*, vol. 25 (June 1969), pp. 7-9, 44-45.

[42] IAEA, "The Structure and Content of Agreements between the Agency and States Required in Connection with the Treaty on the Non-Proliferation of Nuclear Weapons" (INFCIRC/153), as quoted in Willrich and Taylor, *Nuclear Theft*, p. 191. The present study does not cover possible supply of enriched uranium by the U.S. and the U.S.S.R. Israel belongs to the IAEA, but does not participate in its inspection and monitoring program. See statement of Senator Howard H. Baker, Jr., on Israel in Richard L. Homan, "U.N. Assembly Is Cautioned on Efforts to Expel Israel," *Washington Post*, 5 June 1975. Egypt does not take part in the IAEA safeguards program either.

[43] Bell, "Nuclear Option," pp. 126-129. Also see *New York Times*, 19 July 1970.

[44] Prime Minister Yitzhak Rabin, interview with ABC television, 15 April 1975, "Rabin: An Action Biography." He also challenged any implication that Israel had a "secret" nuclear weapons program.

18

political reasons, however, there has been no official admission of actual possession of such warheads.[45]

One must also address the question of the nuclear capability of Arab countries. The only Arab states known to have reactors are Iraq and Egypt.[46] As to the former, there is no evidence of weapons-related work at the Soviet-built reactor south of Baghdad. The Iraqi facility was inaugurated in 1968 [47] and is capable of producing only small amounts of plutonium. In addition, Iraq has concluded a comprehensive NPT safeguards agreement with the IAEA.[48]

The other atomic reactor is the Soviet-built Egyptian facility at Inshass.[49] It is much smaller than the Israeli Dimona reactor [50] (two as compared with twenty-four megawatts), and accordingly its potential is "almost nil." [51] It has been said that, even with a crash Egyptian nuclear weapons program, it would take at least seven to eight years before a locally produced bomb would be available.[52]

More recently, when the U.S. Congress conducted hearings to decide whether a promised reactor should be given to Egypt, testimony varied on how long it would take Cairo, if it chose to do so, to build nuclear weapons. The minimum time estimate was six to ten years.[53] Since the apparent shelving of the American commitments, the French have offered to provide Cairo with a nuclear reactor which will probably take even longer to build. As one expert indicated, if an American reactor would require eight years to build in Egypt, a French one would probably take eleven years.[54]

If in the next decade the Arabs desire to procure an atomic capability, it will be necessary to get one of the established nuclear

---

[45] Rabin ABC interview, 15 April 1975. When asked if Israel had tactical nuclear weapons, the prime minister categorically answered, "No."

[46] *Safeguarding the Atom*, p. 26. Also see *Middle East and North Africa 1972-1973*, p. 376, and Bell, "Nuclear Option," p. 380.

[47] *Middle East and North Africa 1972-1973*, p. 376.

[48] *Safeguarding the Atom*, p. 26.

[49] Jabber, *Nuclear Weapons*, p. 37.

[50] Ibid., p. 35.

[51] *Safeguarding the Atom*, p. 26.

[52] Bell, "Nuclear Option," p. 380.

[53] See testimony by Dr. Henry Kendall, U.S. Congress, House, Committee on Foreign Affairs, Subcommittees on International Organizations and Movements and the Near East and South Asia, *U.S. Foreign Policy and the Export of Nuclear Technology to the Middle East*, 93rd Congress, 2nd session (Washington, D. C.: U.S. Government Printing Office, 1974), pp. 182-183.

[54] Ibid. Testimony by Dr. George Quester, pp. 198-199. In other developments, India's foreign minister reportedly said his country would soon begin talks on possible nuclear cooperation with Egypt. "Crackdown Ordered in Lebanon," *Washington Post*, 30 May 1975.

powers to provide them with bombs or to find some steady supply of fissionable materials. Since the record indicates that the world's nuclear powers have been hesitant to put such weapons under the control of any previously non-nuclear state, the greatest likelihood of the Arab states getting nuclear arms will be via the purchase of civilian reactors, but even then there is no assurance that such facilities will necessarily lead to the development of atomic weapons. Nevertheless, as long as there is no settlement of the Arab-Israeli conflict it is relatively certain that at least some of the Arab states will attempt to procure a nuclear capability to offset an apparent Israeli advantage.

Another form of nonconventional warfare that is potentially disastrous for the Middle East and the rest of the globe is employment of chemical, biological and radiological weapons (CBR).[55] We must consider whether either or both sides have the capability to conduct this type of unconventional war. There is little doubt that the Israelis have the technical manpower base to develop such weapons and, as in the electronic countermeasures field,[56] they may have brought in a number of experts to assist in building up such a capability. Furthermore, the United States has probably provided at least some defensive equipment and possibly—though this is unlikely—even offensive CBR gear may have found its way to Israel.

Here it is important to consider the American Defense Department's conception of what constitutes a good defense against a potential adversary who has chemical and other unconventional weapons. In the past, the argument has usually followed the line that the Soviets may use gases or other chemicals so it is necessary for the United States to have the same or more lethal weapons to respond to any such attack. (The best defense is a strong offense with the same kind of weaponry.) If this is so, then one must consider whether the Israelis have procured such a capability already, in case the Arabs eventually obtain highly sophisticated CBR systems. Of course, a reverse reaction could occur in the sense that, if the Arabs do not already have such weapons, they may be moved to

---

[55] Attention here will be focused on chemical and biological weapons. Radiological dangers may occur either in a nuclear weapons attack or in the use of nonexplosive radiological material in warfare. Radiological weapons of the latter variety, particularly dispersed plutonium of the type abundant in nuclear fuel cycles, are among the most toxic of all substances. No nation is known to have such materials in its arsenal, but concern has been expressed about terrorist use. Willrich and Taylor, *Nuclear Theft*, pp. 10, 24-28. Another designation for chemical-biological warfare is "CBW."

[56] "Eased Export Policy Realization Lags," *Aviation Week and Space Technology*, 21 February 1972, p. 69.

procure them when they think the Israelis have already produced or acquired a CBR capability.

In light of the above possibilities, equipment which was available during the October War takes on added interest since Soviet-supplied weapons gave the Arabs such an extensive capability for defense against chemical, biological and radiological attack that it led United States Army Chief of Staff General Creighton Abrams to refer to it as "one of the most impressive lessons of the conflict." [57] He was quoted as telling the House Armed Services Committee that the army was surprised by the "sophistication, completeness and extensiveness of these defenses." [58] Not surprisingly, this raised the question of why such defenses were provided to the Arabs. Were the Soviets and Arabs worried that the Israelis had an extensive CBR capability and were ready to use it? Or were the Soviets planning to supply their Arab clients with such weapons? [59]

On the Arab side, there is little indication that any kind of indigenous offensive CBR capability exists, although the previously mentioned Soviet-supplied equipment would mean there is an extensive defensive capability. Offensively, the Arabs would undoubtedly have to procure CBR weapons from outside sources such as the U.S.S.R., but there is no indication that Moscow is willing to allow the proliferation of such weapons outside of the Warsaw Pact and Russian control.

In this regard, at least one international expert, Julian Robinson, has already voiced concern over the possible use of weapons such as binary nerve gases in regional wars between smaller nations. Robinson also indicated that "one need look no further than the Middle East to envisage the enormous dangers to world peace of proliferation." [60]

---

[57] John W. Finney, "Abrams Cites Intelligence from Soviet Arms in Mideast," *New York Times*, 15 February 1974.

[58] Ibid.

[59] During the Yemeni war in 1962 Egyptian troops allegedly used some type of poison gas. See "Cairo Said to Use Gas Bombs," *New York Times*, 9 July 1963; and "6 Gas Deaths Listed by Yemen Royalists," *New York Times*, 12 July 1963.

[60] Quotes by John F. Henahan, "The Nerve Gas Controversy," *Atlantic*, September 1974, p. 55.

3

WHAT TYPES OF MILITARY EQUIPMENT IN THE MIDDLE EAST ARE CAPABLE OF DELIVERING NUCLEAR WEAPONS?

In one sense, the question posed by this chapter's title may be taken as meaningless. If there is both the capability and the will to use such means of warfare, does it make any difference *how* they are delivered? This issue has arisen in connection with the relative ease of designing atomic bombs. John S. Foster, former director of defense research and engineering (DDR&E) in the Department of Defense, notes:

> It must be appreciated that the only difficult part of making a fission bomb of some sort is the preparation of a supply of fissionable material of adequate purity; the design of the bomb itself is relatively easy. . . .[1]

A crude fission bomb, therefore, requires little of the sophistication needed to produce the extensive variety of nuclear weapons held by major powers. While there are some who would dispute the conclusion of Mason Willrich and Theodore B. Taylor that key persons responsible for such crude bombs "would have to be reasonably inventive and adept at using laboratory equipment and tools of about the same complexity as those used by students in chemistry and physics laboratories and machine shops,"[2] there is enough widely dispersed technology and equipment to convert even a suitcase into a lethal atomic weapon.

Why worry, then, about the presence of nuclear delivery vehicles—aircraft, artillery, missiles and so on—if one could quite effectively carry out a nuclear suicide mission with little or no military

---

[1] John S. Foster, "Nuclear Weapons," *Encyclopedia Americana*, vol. 20, pp. 520-522, as quoted in Willrich and Taylor, *Nuclear Theft*, p. 7.

[2] Ibid., p. 21.

capability? One should not, of course, rule out such an approach to initiating an atomic calamity in the Middle East, especially among terrorists who have little or nothing to lose.

Taking into account the possibility of constructing atomic bombs for use by irregular forces, it is still more likely that nuclear weapons will be introduced into the Middle East, if at all, by means of sophisticated delivery systems rather than through clandestine terror. While it can be admitted that extremist actions tend to be all too frequent in this region of the world, the fact remains that established governments and their defense ministries are at war. In this continuous warfare between the Arab states and Israel, steadily increasing sophistication of weaponry has developed and been used at escalating stages of warfare.[3] Among such advanced equipment are the weapons of dual capability (that is, both conventional and nuclear) or largely nuclear in design supplied by the United States and the Soviet Union from the same stocks deployed by the North Atlantic Treaty Organization (NATO) and the Warsaw Treaty Organization (WTO). When one couples this supply with shreds of evidence such as the employment of nuclear weapons experts by various Middle Eastern defense ministries, one must face the possibility that regular military uses of nuclear weapons are likely to be the preferred operational strategy of Israel and the Arab states, should decisions to utilize atomic weaponry be made.

The main uses for tactical nuclear weapons, as developed in NATO and the WTO, might also be applicable in the Middle East. Indeed, given the short distances between capitals, "tactical use" on the battlefield could easily be melded into "strategic use" against the enemy's homeland. Again, a suitcase or light plane could deliver crude fission bombs, but in order for nuclear weapons to meet the basic tests for their efficient war-time use as developed by the superpowers, specialized delivery systems are necessary. After examining the central roles of tactical nuclear weapons in Europe, on the assumption these roles would prove substantially similar in the Middle East, the question of what delivery vehicles in the region are most likely nuclear-capable will be addressed. On the latter issue, as with the matter of basic uses, NATO and WTO tactical nuclear strength will be used as a key to possible delivery vehicles presently in the Middle East. Most of these systems come under the rubric of "dual capable," but several appear designed principally for nuclear use. As noted above, almost all of the military equipment in Arab and

---

[3] See Dale R. Tahtinen, *The Arab-Israeli Military Balance since October 1973* (Washington, D. C.: American Enterprise Institute, 1974), p. 1.

Israeli arsenals comes out of Russian and American supplies, the same sources that outfit superpower forces in Europe.

Basic Uses of Tactical Nuclear Weapons

We must first begin with some understanding of the extremely short distances involved in the Middle East. There, what might be termed a "tactical" or "battlefield" atomic system can easily be used against a "strategic" or "homeland" target. Not only could any battlefield be easily extended to cover the enemy's homefront, including its capital city, but any use of nuclear weapons would no doubt be so interpreted, no matter how limited.[4] If such were the case, any attack with nuclear weapons could escalate into not only a local strategic threat but a global one involving the superpowers.

The distance from Tel Aviv/Jerusalem to Damascus is approximately 130 miles by air, or roughly the distance from Washington, D. C., to Philadelphia. Cairo and Tel Aviv are separated by 250 miles, which exceeds the distance from Washington to New York by 50 miles. The entire area of immediate confrontation in the Middle East is located between Damascus and Cairo, which are roughly 375 miles apart. At the extreme edge of Israel's defense worries is Baghdad, some 525 miles away. This area, spanned by supersonic aircraft, missiles and so forth, can be compared dramatically with that of the American Revolutionary War: from Boston to Yorktown, a distance of 450 miles by air, traversed by forces that took a day even to move the few miles from Williamsburg to Yorktown (full, unhindered movement of these forces took roughly three days, 28–30 September 1781). Most combat aircraft in the Middle East are within easy striking distance from one or another of the immediate confrontation areas of Israel, Lebanon, Syria, Jordan, and Egypt. The "deep penetration" raids by Israel's F-4s against Cairo in 1970, as well as Israeli strikes on Damascus in 1973, demonstrate the range of these aircraft as strategic as well as tactical weapons.

Despite the short distances in the Middle East, it is still likely that nuclear weapons, if used at all, will first be employed against approaching forces which cannot be controlled by any other means. The same likelihood would exist in the case of possible use of chemical or biological weapons. This assumption is not based on any

---

[4] Senator Stuart Symington on NATO. U.S. Congress, Joint Committee on Atomic Energy, Subcommittee on Military Applications, *The Consideration of Military Applications of Nuclear Technology*, 93rd Congress, 1st session (Washington, D. C.: U.S. Government Printing Office, 1973), pp. 15-16.

illusions about rational behavior among armed forces in the Middle East, when it comes to the life-and-death views of both sides,[5] but rather stems from the role of the superpowers in the region. Any use of nuclear weapons by the regional combatants would cause anxious tremors between the United States and the Soviet Union, thus raising questions about their joint or unilateral intentions to stop the fighting. Use against military personnel would be bad enough, but atomic attacks of the Hiroshima and Nagasaki type against civilian targets could cause severe response from Washington or Moscow. It would not be surprising, in fact, if warnings about drastic response have not already been issued by the Soviet Union and perhaps by the United States if *any* nuclear warfare should occur in the Middle East. Hence, it is useful to consider the roles of tactical nuclear weapons, from most narrow to most expanded, with the assumption that initial usage in the Arab-Israeli conflict would be strictly local and military. As a somewhat sobering caveat, however, such use of nuclear weapons would most likely come only in a time of extreme desperation when caution would of necessity be abandoned.

Using NATO-WTO deployments as a baseline, the first and narrowest use of tactical nuclear systems is as battlefield or short-range theater weapons [6] used directly against attacking forces.[7] These would have a range of up to seventy miles, with warheads of 0.1 to 2 kilotons. All artillery-delivered nuclear projectiles, as well as certain NATO and WTO missiles and various bombs and bombers, fit this role. As will be seen below, some of this equipment is now in the Middle East, all of it ostensibly in conventional use.

A second use of tactical nuclear weapons, at longer range and with more explosive power, is as long-range theater nuclear weapons designed to influence indirectly combat outcome. Such systems can cover distances of up to 400 miles, with 3 to 400 kiloton warheads. Other NATO and WTO missiles and a number of bombs fall in this category. It is worth noting here that Israel's Jericho missile, devel-

---

[5] On Israel's psychology on the eve of the Six Day War see Brecher, *Decisions in Israel's Foreign Policy*, pp. 333-336. Egypt's President Sadat has recently said: "Guarantees, guarantees for both sides. I need guarantees more than Israel does." Quoted in press statement to Wilson Wynn, FBIS-MEA-75-68, 8 April 1975, p. D 1.

[6] The three basic uses of tactical nuclear weapons are spelled out in Jeffrey Record (with the assistance of Thomas I. Anderson), *U.S. Nuclear Weapons in Europe: Issues and Alternatives* (Washington, D. C.: The Brookings Institution, Studies in Defense Policy, 1974), p. 7.

[7] For example, see Joint Committee on Atomic Energy, *The Consideration of Military Applications of Nuclear Technology*, p. 11, with reference to 155-mm artillery.

oped indigenously, has a range of 280-300 miles. The objective of weapons in this role is to disrupt military activity behind enemy lines—rail junctions, airfields, and so on—but still with battlefield objectives in mind.

The third and final use of tactical nuclear weapons is in a semi-strategic role. For NATO forces this means an ability to strike inside the U.S.S.R. from Europe. America's F-111s and forward-deployed F-4s are involved in this role.[8] In the Middle East, all forms of tactical nuclear weapons could reach certain home-front targets in the confrontation zone. For example, Israeli and Jordanian forces could conceivably trade nuclear fire on each other's principal cities from ground-launched systems, or Israeli and Egyptian forces could fire across the Suez Canal (or close it) in similar fashion. Surely the second category of tactical nuclear weapons can be considered strategic in the Middle East context, while aerially refueled F-4s could operate in a "semi-strategic" mode across the entire Middle East and North Africa.

With these basic uses of tactical nuclear weapons in mind, it is possible to inventory those weapons now in the Middle East that could meet NATO and WTO criteria if they were nuclear armed. It should be emphasized that the earlier discussion was put in terms of basic nuclear technology capabilities and warlike intentions. Neither can be disputed, except in terms of how much evidence is available that nuclear capabilities have been or will be turned to military uses. However, this study must be more purely hypothetical, save for two or three weapons systems in the Middle East which are designed by their makers *primarily* for nuclear use. Nonetheless, the following hypothesis covers the analysis of delivery systems presented below: *if* there is a nuclear capability and the will to use it, *then* these are the kinds of weapons now in the Middle East most likely to deliver atomic ordnance against enemy forces.

Types of Possible Nuclear Weapons and Delivery Systems in the Middle East

In this discussion, emphasis will be placed primarily on those weapons that are used by NATO and WTO forces for delivery of atomic ordnance. The reason for this emphasis is that both sides in the Arab-Israeli conflict are, for the most part, supplied their weaponry by one or the other superpower, and it is quite probable that the

---

[8] See Senator Symington, ibid., pp. 15-16.

parties to the Middle East conflict will adopt a large amount of the military doctrine of their patron states in the area of nuclear planning, much in the way a significant portion of conventional assumptions have been borrowed from the United States and the Soviet Union. Systems used by NATO and Warsaw Pact planners for delivery of nuclear weapons take on additional importance when they also exist in a conflict-prone area outside of Europe.

There is one important point that must be understood when the expression "nuclear weapons and their delivery systems" is used. In the NATO-WTO context, the kinds of systems referred to in this section fall under the rubric of "tactical nuclear weapons," a designation appropriate to the relatively great distances in the European theater of operations. Despite the fact that many large cities lie in any potential zone of warfare in Europe, in certain limited respects one can distinguish meaningfully between a "battlefield" and more general targets. However, Senator Stuart Symington's query, noted earlier, should be recalled, even in connection with Europe, to say nothing of the Middle East.[9] When does nuclear bombing of a capital city, within a zone of combat, cease being a "tactical" move and become a "strategic" one? An intense debate among nuclear experts has risen over this fuzzy distinction: would an escalatory threshold be easily crossed from limited to general nuclear war if tactical nuclear weapons are introduced anywhere in combat?[10]

Moving to the Middle East from the fine distinctions involved in NATO-WTO planning, the use of tactical nuclear weapons in the Arab-Israeli conflict could spell results, for the region and ultimately the world, very similar to the initiation of strategic nuclear war between the United States and the Soviet Union. Given the state of no-war, no-peace, as well as the short distances in the Middle East, the dividing line between tactical and strategic—between battlefield and homeland—would be much thinner than even the precarious

---

[9] Ibid.

[10] See Record, *U.S. Nuclear Weapons in Europe*, pp. 55-70, for discussion of some differences. Record takes a position against further military reliance on tactical nuclear weapons in Europe; indeed, he recommends a reduction "in a manner that preserves European confidence in the United States" (p. 59). For a good statement of the deterrent effect of tactical nuclear weapons in Europe from an official point of view, see testimony of Major General Edward B. Giller, USAF, Assistant General Manager for National Security, Office of the General Manager, Atomic Energy Commission, in Joint Committee on Atomic Energy, *The Consideration of Military Applications of Nuclear Technology*, p. 34. On the overall U.S. tactical nuclear posture in Europe, see Secretary of Defense James R. Schlesinger, *The Theater Nuclear Force Posture in Europe*, A Report to the United States Congress in Compliance with Public Law 93-365 (U.S. Department of Defense, 1975).

threshold in Europe. Nonetheless, as we argued earlier, it is likely that the first introduction of atomic weapons into the Middle East will come via systems designed for short- or intermediate-range tactical nuclear war.

An examination of Table 1 reveals that a significant number of delivery systems available in Europe for nuclear war are also in the arsenals of the states most directly involved in the Arab-Israeli conflict. Indeed, a key factor to keep in mind whenever nuclear systems are discussed is that there are certain types of weapons now in the Middle East conflict that were built *specifically as delivery systems for nuclear weapons.*

Table 1

NATO-WTO NUCLEAR-CAPABLE DELIVERY SYSTEMS
IN THE MIDDLE EAST

NATO	WTO
Ground-Launched	
Lance surface-to-surface missile[a]	Scud surface-to-surface missiles
M-109 155-mm howitzer	Frog-7 surface-to-surface missiles
M-110 8-inch howitzer	8-inch howitzer
Tactical Aircraft	
F-4 (Phantom)[b]	MiG-21 (Fishbed)
Mystere IV-A	MiG-23 (Flogger)
	Su-7 (Fitter)
	Il-28 (Beagle)
	Tu-16 (Badger)

[a] Pending delivery. A sales agreement between the United States and Israel is being held up by the current reassessment of American Middle East policy.

[b] Israel also has so-called "smart bombs," some varieties of which are nuclear capable and tremendously accurate. They are also highly effective in conventional modes. Yet it is most unlikely that the United States has provided any nuclear arming devices to Israel. This last consideration applies to all weapons itemized in this table: the U.S. and the U.S.S.R. have no doubt refrained from intentionally supplying the devices necessary to arm these systems for actual delivery of nuclear weapons. This technology, however, is not beyond the reach of Israel and, perhaps, some of the Arab states, and in case of emergency, the nuclear devices could be readily supplied and installed by the superpowers.

Sources: John W. R. Taylor, ed., *Jane's All the World's Aircraft 1974-75* (New York: Franklin Watts, Inc., 1974); R. T. Pretty and D. H. R. Archer, eds., *Jane's Weapon Systems 1972-73* (New York: McGraw-Hill, 1972); *The Military Balance 1974-75* (London: International Institute for Strategic Studies, 1974); Record, *U.S. Nuclear Weapons in Europe*, pp. 22, 24, 27, 39, 41; and Tahtinen, *The Arab-Israeli Military Balance since October 1973*, pp. 15-16.

Although little information is available about the original Soviet intention for developing the Frog-7 (2–7 series with a range of 4–50 nautical miles) and Scud surface-to-surface missiles (A and B series with a range of 48–185 nautical miles) now included in Egyptian and Syrian arsenals, the majority of Soviet military experts would probably agree that these systems were intended to be used with nuclear warheads in Europe. They are so deployed at this time. They are publicly listed as having dual capability, but is a conventional warhead any more cost effective for these missiles than for the American Lance missile (see below)? [11] Information about American systems can be gleaned from public Department of Defense presentations to Congress. No such open sources exist in the U.S.S.R. On the other hand, Egypt's President Sadat has warned that, if necessary, he will use his surface-to-surface missiles against Israel; he did not specify the nature of their warheads.[12]

With greater certainty (because of public sources of information) it can be said that the American-produced Lance surface-to-surface missile (2.6–70 nautical miles range), which Israel has sought to obtain (a sales agreement between Washington and Tel Aviv is now being held up by the United States, pending reassessment of its Middle East policy), was built for the specific purpose of being used with nuclear warheads.[13] Indeed, Congress even prohibited the

---

[11] Public source is found in Joint Committee on Atomic Energy, *The Consideration of Military Applications of Nuclear Technology*, p. 39.

[12] See Arnaud de Borchgrave interview with Sadat, "Sadat's Vision of the Future," *Newsweek*, 25 March 1974, p. 45. Regarding use of surface-to-surface missiles in the Middle East, there is also an 11 April 1975 interview with Israel's Chief of Staff Lieutenant General Mordechai Gur, by military correspondent Nahman Shai of the Jerusalem Domestic Television Service, in which Gur sees a strong possibility that such missiles will be used in the next round of fighting: "I would say that I assume surface-to-surface rockets will indeed be fired. The moment that the two sides have equipment—and I do not mean unconventional equipment—I think that we should assume they will use it. And hence, we are doing everything that can be done to enable us to face a war of surface-to-surface rockets. Recently there was talk about the possibility that the two sides would refrain from using the surface-to-surface rockets against civilian concentrations. If you ask me I would say that I think this is possible. That is, I think that it is possible to reach a mutual agreement on this subject." Quoted in FBIS-MEA-75-75, 17 April 1975, p. N 4.

[13] Record notes in his table on ground-launched tactical nuclear weapons in NATO that the Lance is *not* dual capable—see Record, *U.S. Nuclear Weapons in Europe*, p. 22. However, one report notes: "A non-nuclear high-explosive warhead has been developed [for the Lance], tested and type-classified by the Army. . . . Even though the non-nuclear 1,000-lb. Lance warhead has not been approved for Army procurement, this would not prevent foreign nations from ordering that type of warhead from the U.S." Clarence A. Robinson, Jr., "Lance Delivery to Israel Expected Soon," *Aviation Week & Space Technology*, 17 February 1975, p. 46.

Pentagon from procuring a conventional warhead for the Lance until such procurement could be proved cost effective, a proof apparently never presented, at least in public.[14] In other words, it was suspected on Capitol Hill that the cost of developing a dual capability for the Lance could not be adequately justified. Nonetheless, it has been reported that when and if the Lance arrives in Israel it will be for use with conventional warheads, presumably including cluster bomblets (CBU) for suppressing anti-aircraft fire.[15] The Lance has been described in these succinct terms by a high-ranking U.S. Air Force officer:

> Lance is mobile, it has its own launcher. You can load it at the fire-site. The Lance is self-propelled and has its own missile on the launcher. It has a [deleted]. It has a very versatile range of 5 to 125 kilometers. They provide [deleted] missiles per launcher on the average. Some launchers may have more or less, depending on the specific targeting, the specific front and the section in which they are located.[16]

Reservations similar to those involving Lance's potential for conventional warheads have already been outlined on the use of Israeli-produced Jericho missiles for non-nuclear use. Cost effectiveness may prove a barrier to conventional usage. If the Jericho is employed in nuclear warfare, then its mission for Israel within the Middle East regional context would be very similar to American reliance on the Pershing 1A surface-to-surface missile in Europe— as a long-range theater nuclear weapons system designed to influence indirectly combat outcome. Together, the Lance and Pershing form

---

[14] U.S. Department of Defense, *Department of Defense Annual Report*, FY 1973, p. 88; FY 1974, p. 73; FY 1975, p. 114. The army is not seeking funds in the Defense Department's fiscal year 1976 budget for the non-nuclear warhead. Robinson, "Lance Delivery to Israel Expected Soon," p. 46.

[15] Ibid. Also, John W. Finney, "Israel to Receive 200 U.S. Missiles," *New York Times*, 24 January 1975. Finney notes: "In some Congressional circles that have been informed of the sale, there is concern that the introduction of a missile known to have a nuclear capability will increase pressures in the region, particularly in the Arab countries to acquire atomic weapons. . . . According to weapons experts, it would not be too difficult for Israel to develop an atomic warhead to fit into the relatively small Lance missile." Apparently this sales case was held up as part of a general Ford administration reappraisal of its Middle East policy after the failure of Secretary Kissinger's 1975 peace mission to the Middle East. See Bernard Gwertzman, "Pentagon Chief Assures Israel of Security Aid," *New York Times*, 24 April 1975; and Geoffrey Godsell, "Israelis Reported Afraid of New U.S. 'Squeeze.' " *Christian Science Monitor*, 23 April 1975.

[16] Testimony of Major General Giller in Joint Committee on Atomic Energy, *The Consideration of Military Applications of Nuclear Technology*, pp. 9-10.

the basic American tactical nuclear missile force in Europe. While the Jericho does not match the characteristics of the Pershing, this 280–300-mile range Israeli missile is capable of complementing the Lance in a nuclear environment.

On the Arab side, there is as yet no missile comparable to the Jericho. Egypt is the only Arab state that has built surface-to-surface missiles, but there is no indication that they are reliable. As early as July 1962, Egypt's late president, Gamal Abdul Nasser, watched the firing of several Egyptian-produced missiles.[17] Cairo's efforts included attempts to develop two single-stage rockets with ranges of 230 and 370 miles and a larger two-stage missile with a range of 425 miles.[18] While at least two of these missiles (assuming the accuracy of range estimates) would have surpassed the Jericho's range capability, they never became operational, although about 100 are said to have been built.[19] In general, the Egyptian program has been a failure, probably due in large part to Cairo's limited scientific base and resulting over-dependence on foreign technicians.[20]

Assuming that the Egyptians will not be able to resurrect their missile program in the near future, and if Cairo desires to match Tel Aviv's advantage in this type of weaponry, then it will be necessary to seek procurement of foreign-made missiles. The most logical source of supply would be the Soviet Union, and in this regard, there are really only two missiles similar to the Jericho that Cairo could even slimly hope to obtain from Moscow.

One of these Soviet missiles is referred to by the NATO code name of Scaleboard. It is reported to have a maximum range of about 425 miles, with a somewhat greater destructive capability than its approximate NATO equivalent, the Pershing.[21] Scaleboard is believed to be operational in the Soviet Union,[22] and there are unconfirmed reports that the missile may be deployed in Eastern Europe.[23] It is not known whether the Scaleboard is dual capable, but it is most likely that its primary mission is nuclear.

The other missile that the Arabs may seek to procure is the Soviet-produced Shaddock, available in naval and land-based versions.

17 Jane's Weapon Systems 1972-73, p. 29.

18 Ibid.

19 Ibid.

20 A. B. Zahlan, "The Science and Technology Gap in the Arab-Israeli Conflict," Journal of Palestine Studies (Spring 1972), p. 25.

21 Jane's Weapon Systems 1972-73, p. 35.

22 Ibid.

23 Record, U.S. Nuclear Weapons in Europe, p. 39.

If the Arab countries were to obtain the naval type, it would give them a new capability vis-à-vis Israel. For example, the Shaddock, with its somewhat less than 100-nautical-mile range and exclusively nuclear capability, could be fitted to the present Whiskey-class submarines now in Egypt's fleet.[24] Such a naval weapon in Cairo's arsenal would make much easier strikes against key Israeli cities and military targets, especially since the launching submarines could stay well outside Tel Aviv's territorial waters prior to any hostilities and yet still be in an excellent launching position. Carried by submarines, the Shaddock would make up in mobility for its inferior range when compared with Israel's Jericho.

Indeed, the role of naval forces will undoubtedly be much greater in any future Middle East conflict, and it could be this possible use of naval weaponry to which Egyptian President Sadat was referring when he answered a question relating to his deterrent capability in the event Tel Aviv were to attack the canal towns. Sadat indicated that if such an attack were to occur, Egypt would retaliate deep into Israel, and when further queried if his answer meant that Cairo would use surface-to-surface missiles, the Egyptian president responded, "Maybe, and maybe by other means." [25] Sadat could have been referring to means other than a shipborne missile attack, but there are few other options available to the Egyptians. At this time, however, there is no hard evidence that Cairo will get the Shaddock missile from the Soviets.

Use of 155-mm and 8-inch artillery for tactical nuclear warfare is well-established in NATO planning. Similarly, WTO forces are armed with nuclear-capable 8-inch howitzers. Improvements (a second generation of shells) are under way in NATO forces to reduce circle of error probability (CEP)—that is, improve accuracy—and to reduce collateral damage associated with the detonation of these artillery shells.[26] Considerable argument exists about the escalatory potential of these weapons. While it is clear that American nuclear laboratories are aggressively pushing a new technology that will

---

[24] John Moore, ed., *Jane's Fighting Ships 1974-75* (New York: Franklin-Watts, 1974), pp. 546, 638. Also see, *Jane's Weapon Systems 1972-73*, pp. 46-49. Thus far the only known replacement of Egyptian Whiskey-class submarines occurred in 1971 when two of these boats sailed from Alexandria to Leningrad and were replaced by two similar types the following year. *Jane's Fighting Ships 1974-75*, p. 101.

[25] Press statement to Wilson Wynn, FBIS-MEA-75-68, p. D 4.

[26] Testimony of General Giller, in Joint Committee on Atomic Energy, *The Consideration of Military Applications of Nuclear Technology*, p. 37.

make tactical nuclear arms "cleaner" and "smaller" [27]—veritable "mininukes"—and that the U.S. Army seems the chief driving force behind this development,[28] little or no evidence exists about whether or not nuclear ordnance used with artillery would lead to an automatic escalation to full-scale atomic war.[29]

What underlies the deployment of nuclear artillery in Europe, as well as its perfection, is something a knowledgeable expert refers to as "a popular theory" of deterrence, which holds that a Russian planner is more concerned about triggering off a U.S. strategic attack which *might* start as tactical nuclear warfare. In other words, it is argued that the Soviet Union is deterred from any attack on NATO, conventional or nuclear, by its uncertainty over NATO's response to such an attack.[30]

If war should erupt in Europe despite this uncertainty, 155-mm and 8-inch nuclear artillery might be used. The 155-mms are deployed forward in army divisions, whereas the 8-inch artillery is located further to the rear. These weapons make possible a rapid response to massed troops and tanks.[31] Indeed, the 155-mm can be moved by

---

[27] Testimony of Dr. Harold Agnew, director, University of California Los Alamos Scientific Laboratory, Los Alamos, New Mexico, ibid., p. 49. He notes: "I know we at Los Alamos have a small, but very elite group that meets with outside people in the defense community and in the various think tanks. They are working very aggressively, trying to influence the DoD to consider using these [deleted] weapons which could be very decisive on a battlefield, yet would limit collateral damage that is usually associated with nuclear weapons."

[28] Testimony of General Giller, ibid., p. 39.

[29] "SENATOR SYMINGTON: We had a running fight for years as to whether or not you could have a tactical nuclear war and hold it to tactical only. Do you have any papers in the Atomic Energy Commission [that indicate] we could have a tactical nuclear war that would not evolve into a strategic effort?

"GENERAL GILLER: No, sir.

"SENATOR SYMINGTON: Is there anything of that character in the Department of Defense?

"GENERAL GILLER: I am not aware of one that addresses the subject in the way you are speaking. There are a lot of studies, you know." Ibid., p. 37.

After laying out the deterrent and war-fighting roles of tactical or "theater" nuclear forces, Secretary of Defense James R. Schlesinger concludes that "these are demanding conditions, and . . . will be difficult to satisfy. . . . We cannot regard our theater nuclear forces as a substitute for powerful conventional capabilities. They have a unique role to play in the spectrum of deterrence. . . . But we cannot lean on them as a crutch in place of a strong non-nuclear leg to the deterrent TRIAD." U.S. Department of Defense, *Annual Defense Department Report of FY 1976 and FY 197T*, 5 February 1975, pp. III-1-3; also Schlesinger, *The Theater Nuclear Force Posture in Europe*, p. 2.

[30] Testimony of General Giller, in Joint Committee on Atomic Energy, *The Consideration of Military Applications of Nuclear Technology*, p. 37; also pp. 11, 34-35.

[31] Ibid.

helicopter.[32] The combination of these two types of artillery is thought to give such tactical nuclear weapons strong deterrent capability in Europe.

Again, the essential question regarding atomic artillery shells, for military planners and politicians alike (and on both sides), "has to do with the question of whether or not tactical nuclear war is a feasible option." Some argue that if war goes nuclear in Europe it will go strategic; others think there should be an "in-between" option.[33] Both schools of thought agree that the primary objective is deterrence within the overall code of nuclear conduct that has evolved between the superpowers. The object is to influence the Soviet or American defense planner whose calculations are fairly predictable under the assumptions of military rationality referred to in Chapter 1.

Returning to the Middle East, Israel is equipped with American-supplied 155-mm and 8-inch howitzers, while the Arab states have Soviet-built 8-inch artillery. It is doubtful that any have been equipped with nuclear shells by the superpowers. But the atomic role of this artillery in a Middle East war would be substantially similar to that in Europe—without any of the alleged benefits of prior deterrence. It would act as a rapid response to massed troops and tanks where it appeared the odds were overwhelmingly in favor of the enemy. What such artillery in the Middle East could not do, and probably would not do even if it were announced that atomic shells were in ground-forces inventories, is provide whatever deterrence against war, conventional and nuclear, is available in NATO and WTO planning. Even in Europe such deterrence may be more fantasy than reality.[34] War is constantly threatening to break out afresh in the Middle East. The likelihood is that nuclear artillery would be used at some extreme point, not in calculated risk of further escalation and surely not in direct communication with an adversary, but out of desperation.

---

[32] Testimony of Major General Frank A. Camm, USA, assistant general manager for military application, AEC, ibid., p. 13.

[33] Ibid.

[34] On the one hand, Harold Agnew, Director of Los Alamos, expresses his belief that "if one had a proper . . . tactical nuclear stockpile [doctrine, one could] . . . deter . . . a war much more effectively [and cheaply] than we have . . . experienced in the last 10 years." Yet on the other hand, Agnew says that perhaps the United States should also have big, Russian-style nuclear weapons because "deterrence is in the eyes of the guy who is going to be deterred. . . . I don't know what deters a person." Ibid., p. 51. Problems with deterrence strategy in Europe are discussed by Morton A. Kaplan, *The Rationale for NATO: European Collective Security—Past and Future* (Washington, D. C.: American Enterprise Institute, 1973), pp. 45-82.

The same considerations of deterrence regarding nuclear artillery in Europe also apply to tactical aircraft carrying atomic weapons. A variety of bombs and stand-off missiles/glide bombs enable aircraft to play a significant role in all three uses of tactical nuclear weapons described earlier. The dividing line between localized tactical air operations and escalation to general atomic war, however, seems even less clear with aircraft than with artillery or ground-launched missiles. An F-4 Phantom dropping a few hundred kilotons of atomic ordnance (many times the Hiroshima bomb) on a city would hardly be seen as a battlefield weapon, even though it is carried in the American inventory as a "tactical aircraft." [35] Indeed, it is not at all clear that the U.S. and the U.S.S.R. have the same definitions for the terms "tactical" and "strategic," thus creating enormous dangers of misperception in case either attacks the other with atomic systems. For the Soviet Union, any nuclear assault against the Russian homeland, even by a "tactical" airplane such as the F-4, would be considered "strategic" war and would portend extreme escalatory dangers, whereas the United States seems to adhere to an organizational distinction between what is "strategically" targeted by the Strategic Air Command (SAC) and in the nuclear triad (land-based intercontinental ballistic missiles, submarine-launched ballistic missiles, and bombers), and what bombs are "tactically" assigned to "fighterbombers" as part of American tactical air strength. [36] As a practical matter, these definitional difficulties have already created fundamental problems in the Strategic Arms Limitations Talks (SALT).

In the Middle East, none of these niceties apply. If European conditions are difficult to separate neatly into tactical and strategic pigeonholes and if superpower arms control measures are plagued with definitional problems, then one can only imagine the discordant perceptions between powers without any direct communication links, to say nothing of rudimentary bilateral relations. President Sadat has vowed that even an Israeli attack on the cities being rebuilt by Egypt along the Suez Canal would be met by Egyptian attacks deep into Israel's heartland, in marked contrast to unanswered air bombardment of these cities only a few years ago. [37] What an air attack using nuclear weapons—or even *threatening* such use—would provoke from either side can scarcely be imagined. In this connection it is worth recalling that the Russians are said to "define strategic

---

[35] Senator Symington, in Joint Committee on Atomic Energy, *The Consideration of Military Applications of Nuclear Technology*, p. 16.
[36] Testimony of General Giller, ibid.
[37] Press statement to Wilson Wynn, FBIS-MEA-75-68, p. D 4.

as anything that can strike the homeland."[38] If Israel were to use its F-4s in a nuclear mode against cities or other vital targets within Arab territory, Moscow might well interpret this strategically—as an attack on its own homeland. The extent of any Soviet "nuclear umbrella" in the Middle East is unknown. Surely any extremist Israeli adventure using aerially refueled Phantoms in attacks on the southern U.S.S.R. would provoke at least threats of Soviet strategic retaliation. In such an event, or perhaps even in the event of an Israeli nuclear strike on Arab lands, the United States would have to make decisions about its own strategic posture. It is obvious, on the other hand, that Israel would interpret an Arab nuclear attack with aircraft and/or missiles as a strategic move requiring awesome retaliation.[39]

---

[38] Testimony of General Giller, in Joint Committee on Atomic Energy, *The Consideration of Military Applications of Nuclear Technology*, p. 16.
[39] Recall the Israeli "Holocaust syndrome" on the eve of the Six Day War—Brecher, *Decisions in Israel's Foreign Policy*, pp. 333-336.

4

WHAT ARE SOME POSSIBLE SCENARIOS FOR THE USE OF NUCLEAR AND CHEMICAL-BIOLOGICAL WEAPONS IN THE MIDDLE EAST?

We have now come full circle. Having answered affirmatively the first question, "Is nuclear war possible in the Middle East?" and then having discussed the possibility that nuclear weapons and launching systems may exist in the region, we can now turn to some possible war scenarios in which these weapons might be used.

Recognizing the inevitable element of fantasy in any discussion about future contingencies, there are ways of controlling it. First, one can spell out certain realistic assumptions underlying these scenarios. Second, the scenarios can be based on analogous, recent military actions by nations with power comparable to states in the Middle East, actions that have involved only conventional force, but in which one can meaningfully imagine the use of nuclear weapons if they had been available. And third, these contingencies will be developed here with Middle East experience in mind.

All the assumptions behind the following scenarios are of the "worst case" sort. It is unlikely that nuclear weapons would be used by anyone out of sheer cunning and with the objective of totally destroying an enemy in a surprise attack (although the preemptive scenario analyzed below might appear to be this kind of action). While the Middle East has had its share of gratuitous terror, this type of violence has been highly specific rather than mass murder. On the other hand, one can assume that nuclear weapons will be used, if at all, out of desperation, and thus, there will be no hesitation to employ them in dire emergencies. In any case, it is most probable that if atomic destruction comes to the Middle East, it will arise from a perceived need for more drastic action than conventional means allow. After Hiroshima and Nagasaki, any further use of nuclear warfare will have to justify itself to world and national opinion. A last-ditch defensive effort would be the best, and perhaps only, such justification. In the most extreme of all circumstances, however, little attention will be paid to apologies.

Recent successful uses of conventional military force by certain powers can provide examples of the kinds of scenarios in the Middle East that might occasion the use of nuclear weapons if such arms are available. In each case, one of the twenty-five "medium powers" of the world was involved, a group of countries that will create many future complications for U.S. defense and foreign policy planners.[1]

North Vietnam's rapid takeover of South Vietnam is our first example. One might call this scenario, from the standpoint of defending against attack, a survival scenario insofar as the issue is one of a last-ditch effort to save one's territorial integrity. Facing a superior opponent, in conventional military terms, Saigon's choices were limited to either negotiated surrender or occupation by the enemy's military forces (with or without a final battle).

A second instance involved the surprise attack by India against East Pakistan in 1971, a well-planned assault that established conclusively Indian military hegemony in South Asia.[2] From the perspective of Pakistan, there was a need to stop or interdict the invasion quickly, something Pakistanis could not do. An effort to mount such a defense could be called an interdiction scenario.

A third and final form of desperate need for defense also occurred during the Indo-Pakistani war of 1971. It involved an alleged Indian plan to destroy Pakistan's forces in the West and conquer Azad Kashmir. Ostensibly, this occasioned movement of the American aircraft carrier *Enterprise* into the Bay of Bengal. If Pakistan's intelligence indicated such an attack was imminent, there would have been a need to head off this devastating blow by preventive action, what one might call a preemptive scenario.[3] Pakistan, of course, had no such preemptive power in conventional terms. It is possible to imagine, therefore, three defensive military scenarios, all arising from some desperate need to stop an enemy possessing superior conventional power: survival, interdiction, and preemption.

Suppose for a moment that South Vietnam and Pakistan had been armed with nuclear weapons, whether or not their enemies also

---

[1] On the "*new, middle power* in the global system" see Brecher, *Decisions in Israel's Foreign Policy*, p. 523; see also Robert J. Pranger, *Defense Implications of International Indeterminacy* (Washington, D. C.: American Enterprise Institute, 1972).

[2] See Wayne Wilcox, *The Emergence of Bangladesh: Problems and Opportunities for a Redefined American Policy in South Asia* (Washington, D. C.: American Enterprise Institute, 1973), pp. 36-43.

[3] Ibid., p. 53.

were. In these two cases, inferior conventional power could be compensated for, in dire circumstances, by initiating atomic warfare. And there can be scarcely any doubt that these countries would have used such weapons had they possessed them. Among the twenty-five medium powers, a number of whom are important actors in regions still very much alive with conflict (which helps explain the advanced military proficiency of some of them), it is likely that unless rather drastic steps to curb nuclear proliferation are taken, a sizeable group will shortly have atomic weapons in their defensive arsenals.[4] With tensions that seem interminable in certain parts of the world, one day these weapons will find actual uses rather than only deterrence roles. If used, they will be detonated in such extreme situations that world opinion will at least be ambivalent, if not sympathetic. It goes without saying that in scarcely any time thereafter the actual employment of nuclear warfare will be legitimized, once its justification is accepted, with serious results for global safety and stability. Eventually the nuclear code between the superpowers will be victimized, unless the U.S. and the U.S.S.R. take steps to forestall atomic war's acceptability among medium powers.

One might shudder at the thought of nuclear war between North and South Vietnam or between India and Pakistan. But India may soon have several atomic weapons and Pakistan will no doubt follow suit, so such thoughts must be entertained. Yet the situation in the Middle East is even more explosive, as far as world peace is concerned, than any of the other major conflicts between medium military powers. And the technological base for producing nuclear weapons exists in the region. Although testing has not taken place

---

[4] See "Nuclear Flat-Earth Thinking," *The Economist*, 23 November 1974 pp. 14-15; Geoffrey Kemp, "Nuclear Forces of Medium Powers," *Adelphi Papers*, nos. 106-107 (London: The International Institute for Strategic Studies, Autumn 1974). "It is the opinion of the author that the current dynamics of the international system are sufficiently uncertain to rule out simple speculation to the effect that further nuclear proliferation is inevitable or, alternatively, that the appeal of nuclear weapons as instruments of national security has irreversibly waned. Conflict over the control of, and access to, scarce resources such as oil has begun to emerge as a key determinant of political alignments. This, in turn, is leading to reevaluations of basic security relationships, especially those between the United States, Western Europe and Japan, and in such reevaluations the question of more independent nuclear options may very well be discussed. For this reason it is considered opportune to examine some of the more basic problems that would face 'Europe,' India, Japan, *or any other entity*, if political decisions to develop nuclear forces were reached." (No. 106, p. 1, emphasis added.) Japan's ruling Liberal Democratic Party backed ratification of the NPT on 25 April 1975, thus clearing the way for ratification by the Japanese parliament. See Don Oberdorfer, "Japan's Chief Party Approves Nuclear Non-Proliferation Pact," *Washington Post*, 26 April 1975.

in the Middle East, it should be realized that no first test has ever failed, and the type of bomb dropped at Hiroshima had never been tested.[5] Nonetheless, the United States and the Soviet Union have supplied some of their most sophisticated weapons to the countries of the region, including certain aircraft, ground-launched missiles, and artillery capable of delivering nuclear bombs, warheads, and shells. Hence, it would not be extreme fantasy to replay the three scenarios of survival, interdiction, and preemption within the Middle East context in order to see what kinds of situations might justify the use of nuclear arms by either the Arab states or Israel.

Survival Scenario

To begin with, we should again take note of a survival syndrome that seems constantly present in the Middle East. For Israel this is expressed as fear of another holocaust similar to that which engulfed over six million European Jews during World War II. A corollary to this fixation is the so-called "Masada complex," a state of mind in Israel that would resist national capitulation until the last defender. It is likely that both fear of the holocaust and the idea of a Masada-like resistance are still very strong in Israeli policy-making circles and public opinion, but there is also a certain amount of self-confidence, born out of victorious military campaigns, that has expressed itself in Prime Minister Rabin's defiance of the United States during Kissinger's 1975 peace mission. While Israeli leaders have voiced objection to American policy in the past (as during the 1969–1971 period of the Rogers plans), it has not been so frankly asserted as during 1975 that Israel would carry out an "information struggle" regarding American presidential policy itself.[6] Not only Rabin's long

---

[5] Willrich and Taylor, *Nuclear Theft*, pp. 5-6.

[6] See Prime Minister Yitzak Rabin: "If we take, for example, the majority of the U.S. public, I believe it will accept and understand Israel's position. Within the administration there are some officials who very much wanted an agreement, whether for Middle Eastern reasons or perhaps for reasons of the situation of the United States in other spheres and areas. . . . I do not think that in the information struggle we are at a disadvantage." Quoted in FBIS-MEA-75-65, 3 April 1975, p. N 4, interview with IDF radio panel, 2 April 1975. See also Rabin on the "two principal levels" of Israel's effort in the U.S.: (1) "a detailed and full-fledged information campaign aimed at the entire American public"; and (2) "the political one . . . to principal personalities of the administration both in the executive and legislative branches." At the second level, "the confrontation is over the content of the relations between the two countries, over the positions of the administration in every sphere, and here we have to demonstrate a firm stand in our position." Quoted in FBIS-MEA-75-77, 21 April 1975, p. N 1, interview with Dov Goldstein of *Ma'ariv*, no date.

tenure in America as Israel's ambassador but his *sabra* (native-born Israeli) background seem to make him less anxious about the holocaust. He knows Israel is stronger militarily than the Arabs, and as chief of staff during the 1967 war he played a major part in his country's most significant victory against its enemies.

From a security standpoint, however, the Six-Day War was in certain respects a poor bargain for Israel. The areas occupied in 1967 became a major focus for Arab anxieties about their own security. What residual holocaust fixation remained in Israel was thus mixed with new Arab fears for their own survival. This explosive mixture reached its most volatile state with the arrival of the first American F-4s in Israel during 1969 and Israel's subsequent deep-penetration raids into Egypt in 1970 with these Phantoms. October 1973 represented the almost inevitable Arab effort to gain some measure of military self-assurance for themselves, even though they were not victorious in any strict sense.[7]

Under present circumstances it is doubtful that survival anxieties are playing the kind of role in the Arab-Israeli conflict that they did until recently. Nonetheless, a new war in the Middle East would probably be interpreted by both sides as something of a final test— like two boxers struggling near the fifteenth round with a feeling that up to this point the match had been a draw. New peace initiatives after a fifth war would be slow in materializing. Israel might well annex the areas occupied in 1967. And the Arabs, sensing this, might become desperate. Fear for survival could then mount rapidly, among the Arabs because of possible Israeli annexation, and among the Israelis because they may think their enemies have given up hope of recovering their lost lands peacefully.

A new Arab-Israeli war, therefore, would be extremely dangerous in terms of the kinds of security anxieties it would release in the Middle East (to say nothing of outside anxiety over, among other things, another oil boycott). Under such circumstances, extreme measures involving nuclear or other unconventional weapons might be used in defense of real or imagined threats to national survival. Almost by definition the fifth Arab-Israeli war would be a sign of extreme bankruptcy on the part of the superpowers and international peacekeeping generally. And it is doubtful that regional combatants would listen to internal or external voices of restraint.

---

[7] A provocative analysis of the October War, from an Arab perspective, is found in Ghassan Tueni, "After October: Military Conflict and Political Change in the Middle East, *Journal of Palestine Studies,* vol. 3, no. 4 (Summer 1974), pp. 114-130.

In a sense, nuclear war could erupt at any time in a fifth round of fighting between Israel and the Arab states because the enemy would be *figuratively*, if not literally, at the capital gates. Indeed, it would not take long before most capital cities and other major population centers in the Middle East would be threatened with destruction, including those in Israel proper. At what point survival might become an issue, thus bringing the survival scenario into play, is anyone's guess, except for those in very high policy-making circles. Here, imagination might prove even stronger than reality; or better put, reality would merge with fantasy.

Interdiction Scenario

It should be recalled that certain tactical nuclear weapons in Europe can be used either to destroy large numbers of an enemy's approaching forces on the frontline or to strike behind lines against rail points, airfields, and so on. Whether used in shorter- or longer-range modes, however, such unconventional arms are designed to slow down or stop a superior conventional attack. Such an attack might come as a surprise or involve a powerful offensive (or counter-offensive) breakthrough, against which retreating forces would have to use some kind of extremely powerful interdiction to turn the tide or at least moderate it.

Middle Eastern wars have seen both surprise attacks and sudden breakthroughs. With the short distances involved and an expected increase in the numbers of tanks and other equipment likely to be used in a new round of fighting,[8] it may prove necessary for either

---

[8] On the point of a more extensive war (though not necessarily tactics) in the next round, both Egyptian and Israeli chiefs of staff agree. See statement to *Al-Ahram* by Egyptian Armed Forces Chief of Staff Lieutenant General Muhammad Ali Fahmi, 22 February 1975, as reported in FBIS-MEA-75-37, 24 February 1975, p. D 1; and interview with Israeli Defense Forces Chief of Staff Lieutenant General Mordechai Gur, 11 April 1975, as reported in FBIS-MEA-75-75, 17 April 1975, p. N 4. Also, Martin Van Creveld observes: "It is a safe guess that the [Israeli] artillery expansion since the [October] war, both quantitatively and qualitatively, dwarfs whatever has been done in other fields. It would seem that the IDF expects its artillery to be able to deal with the hordes of Arab infantrymen that posed such a deadly threat in the October War. To this end, the greatest emphasis is put on cooperation between armour, motorized and mechanized infantry, and artillery." "Arms and the Men," *Jerusalem Post*, 18 March 1975. The foregoing opinions must be placed alongside a more optimistic assessment of the October 1973 War by two western analysts: "Possibly, this part of the Middle East has come to learn, with modern conventional weapons, the same lesson about *de facto* military parity creating stability that Europe once learned with nuclear weapons." Elizabeth Monroe and A. H. Farrar-Hockley, "The Arab-Israel War, October 1973 Background and Events," *Adelphi Papers* no. 111 (London: The International Institute for Strategic Studies, 1975), p. 35.

side to mount an effective interdiction campaign. While one can imagine using conventional means for this, one lesson of the October 1973 War is especially important for the next war, should it occur: equipment and personnel losses were rapid and high, and in a war involving the use of more of everything, attrition should be worse.[9] Even if the superpowers could (or would) mount equipment airlifts on the 1973 scale, this would hardly replenish forces that are larger than they were then.[10] And some doubt may be expressed that even a 1973-style resupply effort would materialize. Whatever the size of an outside assistance effort, attrition would be more rapid than in 1973, given the likelihood that even better sophisticated weaponry is now deployed.[11]

Under these conditions, unconventional options might quickly become attractive if war should erupt again. Given the presence of various kinds of equipment with devices for protection against CBR attack, both sides must expect CBR warfare to be within the capabilities of their enemies. Perhaps the Arabs and Israelis are only imagining things, expecting as usual the worst possible behavior from their opponents. But this expectation would only drive each all the harder to develop its own unconventional options against the possibility that the other might take the initiative. Hence, it is somewhat meaningless to pledge that one's own nation will not be the first to use nuclear weapons (both Rabin and Sadat have so vowed), since all such promises, even if serious in the first place, would evaporate in desperate circumstances. The dictum of Clausewitz, quoted earlier, bears repeating: "In war more than anywhere else in the world, things happen differently to what we had expected, and look differently when near, to what they did at a distance." [12] Neither Egyptians nor Israelis have promised, in any case, *not* to develop unconventional options, whatever their good intentions "at a distance."

---

[9] See Ibid., pp. 32-35. Monroe and Farrar-Hockley think the tremendous loss of expensive offensive equipment to relatively inexpensive defensive arms may herald an era of defensive war in the Middle East at lower monetary costs—the era of the missile taking the place of airplanes and tanks. General Gur, in the interview cited in footnote 8 above, would take issue: "If in the last war some 2,000 tanks clashed in the Golan Heights, the number could be greater in the [next] war. . . . I envisage that the general outline of the war will be very similar."

[10] Tahtinen, *The Arab-Israeli Military Balance since October 1973*, p. 2.

[11] See statement of General Fahmi, cited in footnote 8 above: ". . . there has naturally been an advancement in the quality of arms and the methods of fighting [since October 1973]."

[12] See footnote 7, Chapter 2, above.

One military breakthrough occurred during the October 1973 War that, if the U.S. and the U.S.S.R. had not intervened, might have led Egypt to at least consider more desperate measures if the counter-offensive had continued. This was the Israeli crossing of the Suez Canal in a move to take Suez city. This move would not only have gained Israel more occupied territory, it would have sealed the fate of Egypt's Third Army on the Canal's east bank. Militarily and politically, Egypt could never have accepted these developments. Israeli leaders have subsequently said that American and Russian intervention "saved" Egypt's force in the newly gained narrow Sinai beach-head, and Sadat has stated that he would simply have cut Israel's invading force to ribbons with other conventional forces if he had no other choice.[13] What really would have happened is open to conjecture, but as noted earlier, American military experts were amazed at how much Egyptian equipment had sophisticated CBR protective devices, and one can imagine how Israel's competent forces were outfitted.

In fact, one can say that all of the past four Arab-Israeli wars have shown some form of surprise attack and/or breakthrough which proved decisive to their outcomes. Another round of fighting would no doubt bring other tactical shocks of enormous significance. But this time there may be more desperation in the air, thus providing ground for exaggerated responses to enemy moves that may or may not be purely tactical but could be interpreted in this environment as strategically threatening.

Preemption Scenario

A preemptive move by Israel or the Arab states—what is now called by some "preventive war"—would likely occur when intelligence indicates that an opponent may well strike first, leaving little chance for repulsing the enemy by conventional means. This feeling of inferiority could dictate a preemptive move to prevent such an attack or weaken it. A feeling of inferiority could result for one of two reasons: (1) fear

---

13 Monroe and Farrar-Hockley tend to agree with Egyptian viewpoint, "The Arab-Israel War, October 1973 Background and Events," p. 30; Israeli experts, however, cite the 19 October 1973 speech by as-Sadat where he said, "I cabled President al-Asad [of Syria] to inform him that I did not want to bear the historical responsibility for the destruction of the people of Egypt and the liquidation of its armed forces. I therefore agreed to a cease-fire." For example, see *Der Spiegel* interview with Israeli Defense Minster Shim'on Peres in German, 26 May 1975, as reported in FBIS-MEA-75-105, 30 May 1975, p. N 7.

that one is ill-equipped to stand and fight in the first place, or (2) the fear that one is under-supplied for a long war once started.[14]

Preemption was used brilliantly by Israel's air force in the Six-Day War, in the context of a pervasive holocaust syndrome among Israel's policy-making elite on the eve of that conflict.[15] Controversy raged in Israel after the October 1973 War over why its leadership was surprised by Egypt and Syria, apparently on the assumption that with advance warning Israeli defense forces could have struck first.[16] There is little doubt that the Arab states would do likewise if they expected a surprise Israeli attack, although to date this has not been a preferred Arab strategy.[17]

In a sense, of course, all preemptive or preventive war is a form of surprise attack. Sympathetic analysts of Israel's foreign policy have taken pains to demonstrate that Nasser's closing of the Straits of Tiran in 1967 and his successful effort to remove the United Nations Expeditionary Force from the Sinai were, in essence, acts of war, so that Israel's devastating preemption against Egypt's air force was retaliation, not surprise attack.[18] The effects of a preemptive strike, however, are the same as a surprise attack and will be so treated by the country attacked; both are designed to catch an enemy "by surprise." This might lead to the conclusion that since this will be the final round of fighting and one is already losing after the first shots, one had better take drastic interdictive action against the preemptor. Of course, the

---

[14] Prime Minister Rabin has said that he thinks the question of Israel using preventive war is hypothetical, because he is confident the required military assistance will continue for Israel. This was in response to an interview query about the linkage between preventive war and not receiving enough arms aid: "You said recently that if Israel has the arms it requires it will not need to initiate a preventive war." Interview with Dov Goldstein, quoted in FBIS-MEA-75-77, 21 April 1975, p. N 4.

[15] See Brecher, *Decisions in Israel's Foreign Policy*, regarding Israeli psychology on the eve of the Six-Day War, pp. 333-335, 342-343.

[16] See Terence Smith, "Israeli Study of '73 War Cites Command Failures," *New York Times*, 31 January 1975 (the so-called Agranat Commission 1,512-page final report submitted to the Government of Israel on 30 January 1975).

[17] Answering a question about Israel launching a preventive war (posed by Eric Rouleau and Jean-Paul Peroncel-Hugoz in a *Le Monde* interview of 20 January 1975), President Sadat said: "Yes, I am sure of [Israel's intention to launch a preventive war], because the leaders of the Jewish state are hoping thereby to resolve their formidable internal problems while satisfying the army, which is trying to secure a decisive victory capable of restoring to it the prestige it lost during the last armed conflict. Israeli soldiers did not draw any lesson from the ordeal they suffered. Nevertheless, they ought to be on their guard: *We are as capable as they of resorting to a preventive war if we deem it vital for our defense."* Quoted in FBIS-MEA-75-16, 23 January 1975, p. D 5, emphasis added.

[18] See Brecher, *Decisions in Israel's Foreign Policy*, Chapter 7.

preemptor will probably calculate in advance that the attack will be greeted in this way, and so it will be important that the preemptive attack be so surprising and devastating that no retaliation can be mounted. Any preemptive strike against airfields in today's Middle East with the purpose of producing the same complete effect achieved by Israel against Egypt's air force in the 1967 war, would require enormous explosive power to destroy the kind of sheltering that now protects aircraft on the ground, even if one's attack plan could solve the wide-dispersal, quick-alert, and antiaircraft protection afforded today's Middle East air forces. Using nuclear weapons preemptively, out of fear that one's opponent will attack first and one will somehow be left inferior or that one's enemy might retaliate with his own unconventional means would, for all practical purposes, constitute engaging in a surprise atomic attack.[19]

Any preemptive use of nuclear weapons would not only bring world condemnation but probably retaliation of some sort from one or both superpowers. If Israel were to stage a preemptive strike against the Arabs, the Soviet Union might take drastic action against Israel, with the United States (depending on the nature of the Soviet retaliation) moving in turn against the U.S.S.R. If the Arab states were similarly to attack Israel, the United States might take retaliatory steps, leading to a Russian reaction of some kind.

Preemptive attack with nuclear weapons would surely be the most dangerous use of unconventional arms in the Middle East, with grave repercussions for both the region and the world. Unfortunately, out-and-out surprise and preemption are favored modes of warfare in the interminable struggle between the Arabs and the Israelis.

---

[19] Use of precision guided munitions (PMG) might provide more accurate conventional explosive power. So-called "smart bombs" may improve conventional capabilities, without necessarily being sufficient to destroy, on the ground, the much larger numbers of aircraft in the Middle East today. More to the point, certain PMG can be used in nuclear modes (see Table 1 above).

5
WHAT SHOULD BE THE AMERICAN RESPONSE TO NUCLEAR WAR IN THE MIDDLE EAST?: A FOUR-PART PLAN

Clearly, nuclear war in the Middle East poses a grave threat to the stability and peace of the world. It is only prudent, therefore, that the United States consider in advance its overall posture toward this issue. If such a war should actually occur, it is likely that the nuclear code separating the superpowers and all humankind from a terrible holocaust would itself fall victim. The superpowers may have to consider steps, therefore, to forestall the acceptability of atomic war among medium powers.

Any planned American response to atomic or any other form of unconventional war in the Middle East should take account of all four aspects of the problem previously discussed. First, attention should be paid to third-party use of these means of warfare within the context of the Soviet-American nuclear equilibrium and excluding alliance partners. Are the provisions for such usage adequate to prevent outbreak of unconventional hostilities among medium powers and, if not, is the nuclear code of good conduct between Moscow and Washington strong enough to withstand corrosive forces once medium powers use nuclear weapons?

Second, the matter of technological capability to build nuclear weaponry should be examined. Within existing safeguards, are there ways of rationing this technology? If, at specific levels of national development, scientific and engineering information spreads relentlessly, avoiding efforts to curb it, should the United States encourage this form of cultural exchange? Can progress in the development of nuclear weapons be slowed down, if not stopped entirely?

Third, what attitude should the nuclear superpowers take toward the supply of nuclear-capable military equipment to their respective clients in the Middle East? Within its current security assistance programs, does the United States have the means to tightly control the flow of such delivery systems to medium powers? Should controls be tightened, and, if so, how? What about the feasibility of unilateral and bilateral arms control measures undertaken by the U.S. and the U.S.S.R.?

Fourth, if in spite of every effort at preventing nuclear war in the Middle East it should nonetheless occur, what might be the American response? What kind of contingency planning is necessary for this possibility? Should there be cooperation with the Soviet Union to contain unconventional hostilities within a strictly localized setting? How could such war be stopped once started? What kind of peace-keeping machinery would be necessary in the wake of nuclear war? Should United Nations forces be properly equipped for such circumstances, or is such peacekeeping a job for the superpowers?

The four areas of (1) strategic provision for third-party nuclear war, (2) control of technology, (3) security assistance and arms control and (4) contingency planning for unconventional warfare, provide some framework for a possible plan for an American response to nuclear war in the Middle East. We will conclude by separately examining each of these elements in the plan.

Strategic Provision for Third-Party Nuclear War

The chief danger posed for American interests by nuclear war in the Middle East is the possible erosion and rupture in the U.S.-U.S.S.R. nuclear equilibrium. With this damage to a fragile set of conventions that at once unites and yet separates the awesome strategic forces of the United States and the Soviet Union would come a greater probability of nuclear war between the superpowers.

Within the context of this informal yet highly exacting code of mutual deterrence, the chief governing agreement on third-party nuclear use is the Agreement between the United States of America and the Union of Soviet Socialist Republics on the Prevention of Nuclear War signed by President Nixon and General Secretary Brezhnev on 22 June 1973. Possibly applicable to nuclear war in the Middle East is the following provision in Article IV of the agreement:

> If relations between countries not parties to this Agreement appear to involve the risk of nuclear war between the United States of America and the Union of Soviet Socialist Republics or between either Party and other countries, the United States and the Soviet Union, acting in accordance with the provisions of this Agreement, shall immediately enter into

urgent consultations with each other and make every effort to avert this risk.[1]

What the two superpowers are pledged to do is to meld third-party usage into the crisis-management machinery established between Moscow and Washington to avert nuclear war with each other. In a sense, however, this may be too generous an interpretation. When asked about obligations under Article IV (at a news conference on 22 June 1973), Secretary of State Kissinger specifically ruled out an American role as an arbiter between the Russians and the Chinese:

> What Article IV provides is that if either of the countries contemplates nuclear war with any other country, or of course with the other nuclear country, it has an obligation to consult the other signatory with the purpose of avoiding the situation that would produce such a war.[2]

Apparently, third-party use of nuclear weapons which may *eventually* bring the U.S. and the U.S.S.R. into their own atomic war is not covered by the above interpretation. Indeed, when asked about whether Articles IV and VI obliged the United States to press Israel to sign the NPT, Kissinger responded by refusing to speculate about

> the implications of the agreement on the actions of other countries with respect to existing multilateral agreements. . . . We could not assume that this agreement imposes on the United States a particular additional obligation with respect to treaties whose obligations are already clear.[3]

In essence, then, third-party use of nuclear weapons in the Middle East is poorly covered or not covered at all under the 1973 Nixon-Brezhnev agreement. In light of the Atherton idea of "flexibility" in the American position on the NPT with regard to supplying

---

[1] U.S. Department of State, *Department of State Bulletin*, vol. 69, no. 1778, 23 July 1973, pp. 160-161. Specifically excluded in Article VI(c) are "the obligations undertaken by either Party towards its allies or other countries in treaties, agreements, and other documents." This is an important clause, because its effect is that "third-party usage" will not be construed to mean the use of atomic weapons by alliance partners whose nuclear forces are integrated into the superpower nuclear equilibrium. The status of Middle East countries is murky; President Kennedy apparently assured Israel during 1962-1963 of *de facto* allied status (see footnote 3, Chapter 1); and a 1971 Treaty of Friendship remains in force between Egypt and the U.S.S.R.

[2] Kissinger, ibid., p. 147

[3] Ibid., p. 146. The question was coupled with a reference to a Flora Lewis article that contended that Kissinger "had taken a study by the Rand Corporation on how Israel could attack Egypt with an atomic bomb." Kissinger denied having seen such a study.

nuclear materials in the Middle East, however, it is not even clear that the United States really covers the Middle East under the rudimentary "obligations" of a multilateral treaty (see Chapter 2). It is doubtful, therefore, that any clear American or Soviet understandings exist, publicly at least, on how to behave in bilateral or multilateral terms, should atomic weapons be used in the Middle East.

The serious deficiency of inadequate coverage of third-party use in the nuclear equilibrium between the United States and the Soviet Union should be remedied by some emendation of the 1973 agreement or creation of some new understanding that would clarify the roles of the two superpowers toward a conflict where nuclear weapons were used by medium powers with potentially serious consequences for relations between Moscow and Washington, but where, in the war's early phases, neither superpower was directly involved. In turn, the extension of the nuclear umbrellas of the U.S. and the U.S.S.R. over medium powers with their own nuclear weapons potential should be carefully considered and generally avoided, except for alliance partners already integrated into the strategic balance.

Control of Technology

The discussion of laser isotope-enrichment of uranium in Chapter 2 demonstrates the difficulty of rationing the export of technology among nations with comparable scientific development. Similarly, the building of nuclear weapons is a technology available to scientifically advanced groups worldwide. Having granted in principle the transfer of technology among cultures of roughly similar scientific expertise, however, one need not extend the same parity in practice. Nuclear technology is notoriously expensive, so that nations with highly trained human resources but low gross national products are not likely to be investing in major atomic weapons programs without significant outside assistance. Hence, Canada found itself being misled by India's "peaceful" applications of atomic energy, or so the Canadians alleged after India exploded its first nuclear device in 1974. Most Middle Eastern countries, including all the parties directly involved in the Arab-Israeli conflict, have annual incomes already over-committed to national defense for conventional arms. Of course, since there are few public facts about the structure of defense budgets in the Middle East, it is impossible to determine from open sources just how military funds are allocated and spent. No doubt any expenditures on nuclear weapons would be highly classified. Nevertheless, one can assume with some assurance that a sound nuclear weapons program for any Middle

Eastern state will demand a good deal of outside assistance, ranging from the many exchange visits between citizens of superpowers and citizens of client states to the numerous subventions for defense that go under the heading of economic and military assistance programs.

In principle, then, technology will spread through cultures of relatively comparable scientific standing, but in practice the capabilities of such cultures for turning something like nuclear competence into an atomic arsenal are limited. As noted earlier, very few nations or groups would be hard-pressed to put crude fission bombs in some sort of homemade delivery system, but the distance from this essentially terrorist activity to sophisticated military competence is a long one.

The superpowers should reevaluate and constantly assess those exchange programs which might contribute to giving "free" nuclear weapons technology where otherwise it would be quite expensive. In addition, their security assistance programs should be examined from the standpoint of what areas of a national defense budget are being contributed to. In this connection, the United States and the Soviet Union should have a clear, detailed picture of the military budgets of their clients in the Middle East. Finally, the supply of nuclear materials and equipment should be carefully monitored under existing multilateral agreements, with little or no room for "flexibility" in applying NPT standards to the Middle East.

The Economist has, perhaps, put the matter in its clearest perspective:

> No legalistic quibbling should be allowed to obscure the fact that parties to the treaty are pledged to supply no nuclear materials or equipment to countries that have not accepted full NPT safeguards on all their nuclear activities. This pledge has been flouted—and negotiations now in progress suggest an intention to go on flouting it. Prominent among the offending suppliers have been Canada and the United States, which are parties to the NPT, and France, which is not a party but has formally promised to act as if it were one. Prominent among the current or prospective beneficiaries are Egypt, India, Iran, Israel, Japan and South Africa. The deals made between these partners are all, of course, said to be of a tremendously peaceful nature—and, of course, they all swell the flood of plutonium.[4]

---

[4] "Nuclear Flat-Earth Thinking," p. 15. Elsewhere, Jozef Goldblat, of the Stockholm International Peace Research Institute, makes note of the following argument: "While a case could be made for some extension of the delay for the conclusion of the IAEA safeguards agreements by the parties to the NPT, in

Security Assistance and Arms Control

The magnitude of attempting reappraisal and control of sophisticated delivery systems capable of carrying nuclear weapons is perhaps best illustrated by a note in *Aviation Week & Space Technology* of 28 April 1975 to the effect that

> Israel is attempting to generate domestic political pressure in the U.S. to break the Ford Administration's hold on the sale of McDonnell Douglas F-15 fighters and LTV Aerospace Corp. Lance battlefield missiles. Congressional pressure both from Jewish ethnic groups and the aerospace industry is being sought. *Israeli officials last week pressed McDonnell Douglas to enlist its Washington lobby to obtain release of the F-15s but were refused by the company.* . . . Israelis believe that objections from the State and Defense departments to providing F-15s and Lances can be overruled in Congress.[5]

Realistically, most security assistance decisions on the Middle East are a matter of timing rather than categorical refusal. The most famous "reappraisal" of American arms policy toward the region—prior to the one now being undertaken by the Ford administration—occurred in early 1970 when the United States was trying to couple Israel's request for more A-4s and F-4s to the peace initiatives spearheaded by Secretary of State William P. Rogers.[6] The timing approach

view of their formal commitment to non-proliferation, there is no excuse for doing so with respect to nonparties. In the light of these arguments, the recent accords on U.S. nuclear supplies to Egypt and Israel, neither of them party to the NPT or to IAEA safeguards agreements applying to all peaceful nuclear activities, appear as a breach of the NPT." He concludes by stating that the "fragility of the NPT" is mainly due to the fact that the parties, "especially the nuclear-weapon parties," have not fulfilled their commitments under the treaty. "The Indian Nuclear Test and the NPT," in Anne W. Marks, ed., *NPT: Paradoxes and Problems* (Washington, D. C.: The Arms Control Association and Carnegie Endowment for International Peace, 1975), pp. 35, 39-40. Quite obviously the U.S. Department of State does not agree with the idea that supply of nuclear materials to non-NPT states in the Middle East constitutes a breach of the NPT. Also, note Thomas O'Toole, "S. Africa Gets A-Bomb Type U.S. Uranium," *Washington Post*, 14 April 1975; and David Burnham, "New Curbs Urged on U.S. Nuclear Sales Abroad," *New York Times*, 24 April 1975 (with reference to recommendations by Rep. Les Aspin, D-Wis.).

[5] In "Washington Roundup," *Aviation Week & Space Technology*, vol. 102, no. 17 (28 April 1975), p. 15. See also Bernard Gwertzman, "75 Senators Back Israel's Aid Bids," *New York Times*, 22 May 1975. The number finally became seventy-six.

[6] See Brecher, *Decisions in Israel's Foreign Policy*, Chapter 8, and Robert J. Pranger, *American Policy for Peace in the Middle East 1969-1971: Problems of Principle, Maneuver and Time* (Washington, D. C.: American Enterprise Institute, 1971), pp. 23-28.

does not rule out a total embargo or even a partial one, but it is likely that any such steps would be considered too drastic by one super-power if the other did not follow suit. Under highly unusual circumstances, however, where one or another Middle Eastern state might deliberately thwart the cause of peace for its own aggrandizement, and to the detriment of one or the other of the nuclear giants, one might imagine such a unilateral arms embargo.

This study, however, has concentrated on realistic possibilities, and the unilateral embargo option, while feasible, is extreme for a number of reasons including the political one alluded to in the article quoted above. With reference to nuclear delivery systems, most security assistance policies will fall somewhere between promiscuity and continence. And it will be likely that any long-term controls on the supply of such systems will be better sustained as bilateral agreements between Moscow and Washington rather than as one-sided gestures.

Elsewhere, one of the authors of this study has recommended a scheme for arms control in the Middle East that incorporates both unilateral and bilateral measures by the United States and the Soviet Union.[7] In another publication, the co-authors have dealt with methods for understanding, strengthening, and limiting military assistance programs.[8] Drawing from these previous studies, the following recommendations for controlling the flow of nuclear delivery systems into the Middle East are made.

The United States can tighten its control procedures by regularizing high-level review, including presidential decision making, of all major items that might contribute to nuclear-capable military equipment in the Middle East. This review would encompass artillery as well as surface-to-surface missiles, aircraft, and maritime systems (see Chapter 3). In addition, on a unilateral basis, the intelligence community should be assigned to monitor all such equipment now in the Middle East, even that which appears entirely devoted to conventional use.

As a bilateral measure with the Soviet Union, the United States should propose an agreement of finite duration that would prohibit introduction into the Middle East of any launch vehicle that has not been totally stripped of special devices for use with nuclear ordnance. In addition, both superpowers should watch closely technological exchanges (including technical manuals and briefings) that might yield

[7] Robert J. Pranger, *Towards Arms Control in the Middle East*, Middle East Problem Paper No. 9 (Washington, D. C.: The Middle East Institute, 1974).
[8] Robert J. Pranger and Dale R. Tahtinen, *Toward a Realistic Military Assistance Program* (Washington, D. C.: American Enterprise Institute, 1974), pp. 10-28.

valuable information on how to construct nuclear arming devices for certain systems. Ordnance, such as "smart bombs" that could be converted to tactical nuclear use, should also be carefully controlled through bilateral agreements.[9]

Contingency Planning for Unconventional Warfare

We noted at the end of the preceding chapter that a nuclear scenario involving preemptive or preventive war would cause special strains on the U.S.-U.S.S.R. nuclear equilibrium. The other scenarios discussed above would also generate tremors between Moscow and Washington. While a formal agreement, such as an amended Article IV in the 1973 Nixon-Brezhnev agreement on preventing nuclear war, would be highly desirable, there is probably no substitute for contingency planning by the superpowers for dealing with atomic war in the Middle East.

What should the United States do? From the standpoint of advance planning, there are probably two forms of appropriate American action, each related to a particular set of circumstances. At the outset of any nuclear war in the Middle East, the superpowers should work to contain the area of such fighting to the most restricted scope possible. This is another way of saying that a set of contingencies should involve isolating the combatants so that the effects of their warfare do not spread to wider regional populations and to the Soviet-American nuclear equilibrium.

A second group of contingencies has to do with stopping a nuclear war once it has started. While containing a Middle East nuclear war would involve United States and Soviet forces on the periphery in high alert status and yet in continuous contact with each other, ending such a war would require these same powers—separately, together, under the United Nations, or in some combination of these possibilities—to intervene, end the fighting, and move the parties back to prewar positions. A special kind of peacekeeping force will have to enter the picture, one equipped to handle defenses against tactical nuclear war and to administer medical and other programs in radioactive environments. It is likely that only American and Russian forces are equipped for this in any depth, which raises

---

[9] These prohibitions might also include visits to certain American military installations, laboratories, and private production facilities by offical representatives and other citizens from medium powers. While such restrictions have. been most often applied to persons from Communist countries, they might also include states with nuclear weapons potential—if it is not already too late.

the issue of unilateral or bilateral peacekeeping units rather than the usual U.N. contingents, which do not include superpower units.[10] For contingency planning, therefore, the following steps are recommended.

The United States should prepare unilaterally and in consultation with the Soviet Union for possible nuclear war in the Middle East, the consultation being on an informal, low-key basis. Included in such preparation should be contingency planning for severely isolating the zone of atomic warfare and for terminating unconventional hostilities at the earliest possible date. Conflict termination would require full-scale preparation of an American peacekeeping force, perhaps in cooperation with a Russian one, capable of dealing with all aspects of an environment ravaged by nuclear weapons. Such destruction may be limited and involve but a few casualties, or it may cover an extensive area with many persons affected. Given the short distances in the Middle East, there is every likelihood that nuclear war, even if confined to the "battlefield," would quickly encompass large population centers and numerous noncombatants. Without the suggested contingency planning, however, nuclear war in the Middle East could well spread to world atomic war, a wildfire whose only containment would come when it devoured itself.

---

[10] Over the past two years there have been suggestions from the Department of Defense that the use of nuclear weapons by third powers can somehow be countered by the United States under more flexible nuclear options of its own. Implicit in this approach is the belief of American defense planners that the United States can either deter such usage or actually fight wars against nuclear powers other than the U.S.S.R. and the P.R.C. Perhaps this has to do with problems of containing and terminating conflicts between medium powers involving atomic weaponry. The idea is unclear but interesting. See Secretary of Defense James R. Schlesinger, U.S. Department of Defense, *Annual Defense Department Report FY 1975* (4 March 1974), pp. 28, 38; *Annual Defense Department Report FY 1976 and FY 197T* (5 February 1975), p. II-2.

Cover and book design: Pat Taylor